REDISCOVERING THE ANGELS

Other books by the author:

THE JOURNEY UPWARD

INSIGHTS INTO REALITY

THE KINGDOM OF THE SHINING ONES

GATEWAYS INTO LIGHT

THE DRAMA OF INCARNATION

THE MEANING AND VALUE OF THE SACRAMENTS

DISCIPLINES OF THE HOLY QUEST

SONGS OF DELIVERANCE

THROUGH LENT TO RESURRECTION

THE SACRED HEART OF CHRISTMAS

THESE, TOO, SHALL BE LOVED

TRAVEL WITH INNER PERCEPTIVENESS

Biography of the author:

SONGS FROM THE HOUSE OF PILGRIMAGE
    by Dr. Stephen Isaac

Accounts of the author's effect on individual lives:

THE GATHERING OF SOULS
    edited by Clare Carr and Iris Freelander

A SOLAR ANGEL   DONALD E. BURSON

REDISCOVERING THE ANGELS

COMBINED WITH NATIVES OF ETERNITY

BY FLOWER A. NEWHOUSE

THE CHRISTWARD MINISTRY
RT. 5, BOX 206
ESCONDIDO, CALIFORNIA 92025

REDISCOVERING THE ANGELS
© 1950, 1966, 1976 BY
THE CHRISTWARD MINISTRY
ESCONDIDO, CALIFORNIA

ONE EDITION

NATIVES OF ETERNITY
© 1937, 1944, 1965 BY
THE CHRISTWARD MINISTRY
ESCONDIDO, CALIFORNIA

FOUR EDITIONS

SEVENTH COMBINED EDITION

ISBN 0—910378—02

PRINTED IN THE UNITED STATES OF AMERICA

Dedicated directly to those living, luminous ones whose consciousness embraces infinity, yet whose services include things finite. If those who read these pages will realize more love and reverence for these eloquent emissaries, we shall feel that a small measure of our human obligation to them will have been joyously met.

CONTENTS

Rediscovering the Angels

Natives of Eternity

ILLUSTRATIONS

Rediscovering the Angels

Natives of Eternity

FOREWORD

WITHIN the last decade we have heard repeatedly the term "One World." Events seem to be shaping themselves into a creation of not only a "one world" consciousness but a single world federation. Something of the same change toward simplification and unity is noticeable on the inward planes of consciousness—those levels aspired to by philosophy and religion. Men are being awakened to realities of being and principle more universally than in any time previous in the long history of this world. Life is moving men and affairs, in ideals as well as in efforts, toward a remarkable unity. Only the outlines of a vast integral change are now perceptible; but already they suggest the further alterations which are to follow. During the next fifty years, mankind shall not only work, but be *impelled*, to erase national, racial, religious and social boundaries.

Similar internal pressure will urge men to pioneer beyond territories which religion, philosophy and psychology now embrace. They will enter fields of investigation and discovery which were known only to Adepts, seers and mystics until this universal revelation.

One of the renowned realities to be rediscovered by multitudes pertains to the Angel Kingdom. A recognition of the Angels has always been activating a score of the nations and the religions of the earth. Now, however, we are entering an era when the existence and activities of Angels will be accepted almost as readily as is the existence of the Infinite Spirit of God. The trend in this direction is noticeable in present day literature.

In this volume I write of beings who are not figures in the realm of my belief, but rather, known presences within the inclusion of my *certainties*. The Angels are just as fully a part of my consciousness as are my family and friends.

Next to worship and realization of God and the Lord Christ, awareness of the Angelic Kingdom has helped and inspired me more than any other single reality my recognition has touched. Both in individual and group endeavors, and either as a recipient or an observer, I have beheld their wondrous works. In times of crisis, Angel Visitants have enlightened, healed, or aided me in ways too sacredly personal to relate. Because they have contributed so inclusively to what I have gathered as certainties, I have pledged my life to adding what small treasure of knowledge I have gathered to the world's general awareness of their reality.

What stimulus we gain in realizing that our slowly unfolding natures are supervised not only by illumined members of our own human kingdom, but by vivacious, selfless watchers of Angelic Orders! An earthian who merely seeks his own mastership, or an attainment of prodigious knowledge, seems to labor in a rather incomplete inner world. Let him add to his self-conquest a conscious awareness of bright, loyal companions whose range of spirituality far exceeds his own, and his inward world will be infinitely more interesting and spacious, as well as truer in relation to actuality.

When we add the Angel Kingdom to our already accepted beliefs of man's growth into Mastership amidst the influence of eternal laws, we have augmented and enlarged our realization of spiritual beauty within vibrant, pure forms. We have everything to gain from such reverent inclusion! In time we shall feel as deep a bond with Angelic Orders as we do with our own human kingdom; and from this loving fusion of spiritual oneness will come a powerful unity—the nucleus of even more glorious unfoldments to be achieved.

FLOWER A. NEWHOUSE

IN EXPLANATION

WE are combining our first two books on the Angels, *Rediscovering the Angels* and *Natives of Eternity*, into one volume.

The pictures in the first section are done by Jonathan Wiltshire and Donald Burson. These artists receive impressions of these beings intuitionally. When such pictures are complete, I identify the specific order and service of the one they inwardly beheld. The difficulties of transposing the brilliance and vitality of holy ones are enormous. Though transition from the inner realms into visual two dimensional forms causes a loss of beauty and accuracy, enough of reality remains to help us realize in part, at least, the sacred loveliness of the shining ones who perpetually surround us.

In the second section of this volume, Miss Mildred Compton is the artist. A natural question which arises in the minds of those who study the pictures is, "Are these faces idealistic conceptions of Angels or are they authentic likenesses?" They are embodied in this text *only* because these illustrations are good resemblances of the types of beings mentioned in this volume. Miss Compton has glimpses of these beings at times when she is in a very high state of attunement. She is not always aware of the kind of life she discerns. Each of the paintings she has brought forth, that I have seen, represents a definite server or order.

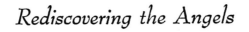

Rediscovering the Angels

THE REALITY OF ANGELIC HOSTS

HUMAN BEINGS are not God's only creation. To know something of His other orders expands the circle of our enlightenment. The very opening of man's mind to the sunlight of truth will increase his yearning for and appreciation of the "Couriers of Heaven." Knowledge of the Angelic Kingdom imparts added comfort, faith and reverence to our thoughts. Between the silent, immutable perfection of God and unfinished, imperfect man stand the Angels—anointed emissaries of the will toward goodness, wisdom and perfection. Their invisible influence works constantly to restrain and purify evil and to awaken dormant good in all things.

"Angel" is the Greek word for a *messenger, one sent,* and is used generally to indicate the "ministering spirits" sent out as messengers of God. (The Hebrew word, translated "Angel," has the same meaning.) God does not require Angels to assist Him, but He employs their services for the sake of their own development. Man's worship belongs to God and His perfected Son, the Christ. His prayers are ever and only addressed to the Supreme Source of all Good. The Angels do not seek or want our homage, but only our love, trust and respectful cooperation in carrying out the Will of God in ourselves on earth.

There has always existed a belief in the Kingdom of Angels. Numerous references to these great benefactors of mankind are to be found in nearly all the sacred books of world religions. Knowledge concerning the

17

Angelic Kingdom has belonged to the archives of humanity since primeval receptions of great truths. This has been one of the few basic revelations that has been the least distorted and changed. We need its full import of blessings, even as we need to learn of the realities of all gradations of glorious life that the Supreme Spirit has invested with Himself since time unfolded God's purposes. It is not logical reasoning to presume that because God does not *need* Angels, they therefore do not exist; for God does not need man, yet man exists!

Those whose spiritual insight has penetrated beyond physical barriers realize that Angelic Beings evolve as do men, slowly and gradually until at last they too enter the supernal glory of unity with God's everlastingness. Because they are more advanced than men, Angels know more of the mysteries of life than we do as yet. While they serve purely, joyously and selflessly in mood and action, a portion of their consciousness is perpetually adoring and contemplating the Presence of God.

For example, were we spiritually awake, we should observe the verdure of the earth peopled by nature beings, exquisitely small and dainty, moving in harmony with the soft, diffused music of the heavens. Forests and mountains, thought to be lonely and uninhabited, would be known to be populated by many tall, graceful beings who hover over trees, lakes and hillsides.

A recognition of other orders of life has always been within the possession of man. Primitive peoples responded to superphysical realities very naturally, but added to truth their own embellishments born of their fears, exaggerations and conflicts. Ancient peoples accepted Angels as they accepted sunshine and to each they

accorded their own meanings. Due to the limited understanding of primitive minds, Devanic manifestations
were accorded positions and powers which were sometimes outside their province. Despite childish, fanciful
and inaccurate accounts of this *other line of God-life*,
within humanity's myths and legends we find flashes
of reality which greatly enrich our understanding of the
activities of the Shining Ones.

One source of acquaintance with elementals or Angelhood stratas of development springs from the racial and
religious interpretations concerning these evolving Angelic Orders. The evolution of Angels is lengthy and
complex indeed, compared to the evolution of human
beings. Some phase of their hierarchal service and mode
of growth is perceptible in nearly all of the religious beliefs of the world. Our endeavor shall be to separate
truth from myth, the kernel of reality from the cum-
bersome husks of tradition. Out of these separations we
shall glean kernels with which to nourish a much more
inclusive and extensive comprehension of the wondrous
range of God-life.

Those races and religions which especially accepted
the reality of Angelic visitants were the Egyptians, Romans, Greeks, Persians, the Muslims, Japanese Shintoists, Jewish Kabalists, the Hindus, and the Maoris. Both
the Old and the New Testaments of the Bible give tribute to the existence and selfless service of the Angels.
We find much regarding them in Daniel, Isaiah, the
Psalms, Revelation and Acts. The deep teachings in the
Jewish Kabala accord the Shining Ones frequent and
reverent mention. Of the Apocryphal writings, the
Books of Enoch include these beings more than do any

of the other ancient scripts. Angels were as naturally accepted as was the existence of human beings by some of the greatest thinkers and writers of the ages: Socrates, Plato, St. Augustine, Jerome, Gregory, Hugh S. Victor, Dionysius, and the later initiates, Paracelsus, Thomas Moore, William Blake, Milton, Edwin Arnold, and Shakespeare.

Much of mythology contains prisms of the White Light of Truth. The ancients understood that various idyllic abodes of men, Devas and Angels, such as Arcadia, Olympus, Elysium, Valhalla, Nirvana and Paradise, actually referred to definite locations of infinite beauty and specialized power. Legends concerning Mt. Olympus, the tallest mountain peak in Greece, signify that it is what was claimed for it, a habitation in the higher dimensional spaces of Angelic radiation. The Turkish peoples named Mt. Olmypus the "Abode of the Celestials."

Enlightened thinkers of past centuries believed in Angels either as a result of their intellectual conclusions, or because they had had experiences of contact with the bright messengers of higher dimensions. Some of the more profound of these thinkers were Pythagoras, Tertullian, Homer, Thales, St. Thomas Aquinas, Jacob Boehme, and Swedenborg. The Bible abounds in references to these celestial natives, as will be noted in the list appearing later in this volume.

Scholars today mention how earliest peoples personalized the elements and deified them. This was due to the fact that unsophisticated minds sensed powers affecting their lives that were beyond the scope of their perceptions. When the Matchless Creator formed man He

20

gave the guidance of humanity into the keeping of Intelligences comparable in intellect and purity to those of the great Avatars who helped establish men on earth.

Mankind was not a mass of purposeless matter, but an order of especially created life whose objective was clarified and stimulated by minds who directed the slow, painstaking course of evolution. Ancient man believed that since his moral and cultural developments were incited by benign intelligences, in a like sense, *all of life must have purpose and intelligences supervising that purpose.* Moreover, he beheld nature as influenced by aerial hosts, busy in executing the will of the Supreme Creator. Everything which was made—earth, water, fire and air—moved to invisible commands of benign or malefic powers. Instinctive within primitive man was a dim recognition, however clumsily expressed, that beneficent growth depended upon some mysterious harmonizing of all the forces of being. He innately concluded that chaos, earthquakes, plagues and wars were the outbreak of unholy energies intent upon delay or destruction of the work purposed by the Divine Will.

Since human beings constitute only one line of evolving life—actually only a small fraction of the whole design of Divine Creation—we should realize that the Creator would have as great an interest in one of His creations as in another. Why, then, should men find it difficult to conceive beings within the elements as natural to their environment as man is natural to earth? Some vague recognition of this possibility in previous races introduced the worship of multiple deities. To this partial cognition of a great reality, man gave the devotion of his primitively fearful, superstitious and ignorant

21

temperament. Thus were the splendid realities, twisted by human distortions, made less able to function in their true and full role for the welfare of mankind.

Through the light of modern esoteric research let us review some fragments of reality which these earlier peoples discerned. To them every aspect of nature was activated by superphysical deities: the air was inhabited by ethereal presences who had charge of clouds, storms, rain, wind and the weather. Even the winds were named and designated as friendly or unfriendly. The intelligence who ruled the north wind was known as the benevolent Boreas. Destructive winds were called Harpies and Furies. They were even distinguished by the malefic messengers, Stormswift and his brother, Swiftfoot. The head of the Wind Beings was given the name Aeolus. The Greeks associated Hermes with the Air Kingdom, believing him to be Lord of the Clouds. The Egyptians believed Enlil presided over storms, while Thor became the Thunder-God of the Norsemen.

A great blessing to mankind for all time will be the recognition of the inner reality of all Angelic Life, and that the worship of God in every kingdom is natural. Even the builders of nature's forms forever strive toward those expanding attainments in consciousness and power which are summarized in the Lords of their realms. In nature's kingdom are advanced overseers of the activities of the out-of-door world. The Angels of this line of evolution are far more advanced than most humans. Their radiations are selfless and joyous. They constitute vivacious presences who ray out vitality and electric energy.

One specific line of evolution, known as *nature ele-*

22

mentals, have bodies composed of the elements in which they live. The more highly unfolded, the more ethereal they appear. For the sake of clarity, four classifications of nature beings can be distinguished:

1. *Air:* Fairies are an elemental creation of the air evolution. Sylphs reveal a more evolved degree of progress. At all times of the day the happy sylphs of the air may be discerned, busy in their lyrical activities above earth's countryside. Advanced orders of this kingdom are found in rulers of the winds and clouds.
2. *Earth:* Gnomes, brownies, pixies, dryads, wood nymphs are a few designations given earth spirits or intelligences developed through the etheric emanations of the earth.
3. *Water:* Water sprites (or water nymphs), naiads, undines were referred to in myth and legend from time primordial as the etheric citizenry of water.
4. *Fire:* Salamanders represent residents of the fire kingdom having perhaps the least association with men of all the elementals.

It is interesting to note, in a few references to these nature beings in ancient myths, legends and folklore, reflected gleams of truth which influenced the thinking of earlier peoples. For example, to the Greeks, the sylphs of the stratosphere became the Muses. Their loftiest ruler, Peralda, dwelt in the region above the peak of Mt. Olympus. To the sylphs the ancients attributed as one of their duties the control of vapor and gas. It was surmised that they also exerted a helpful influence upon man's nervous system. A most interesting duty believed to be assigned to these inhabitants of the air was that of

23

designing the patterns of snowflakes. Paracelsus claimed from his own investigation that beings which were advancing through the air kingdom were noticeably constant and faithful; that water beings were expressive of self-control; earth spirits inclined toward unselfishness; and fire beings radiated outstanding sincerity and purity.

Plato makes known Socrates' perceptions of Devanic ministrations. To this noble Grecian sage is attributed the observation, "And upon the earth are animals and men. There are others dwelling in the air. . . In a word, the air is used by them as the water and sea are used by us. Moreover, their temperament is such that they have no disease. . . They have sight, hearing and smell, and all the other senses in far greater perfection than we, in the same degree that air is purer than water, or ether than air. Also, they have temples and sacred palaces. In these the gods really dwell whose voices they hear and whose answers they receive, and they are conscious of them and hold converse with them. They see the sun, moon and stars as they really are, and their other blessedness is of a piece with this."

A present day believer in the intelligences of the air is George Russell, the Irish poet, known familiarly as "A.E." On a vacation to the seacoast he met a group of sylphs who became his friends. Whenever he returned to that particular site he was reunited with his "friends of the air." On the walls of his study in Dublin he hung murals that pictured these sylphs whom the poet knew and loved.

The seers of the past found an infinite variety of beings in the etheric, superphysical structure of nature.

24

They observed them in the grasses, trees, gardens and mountains. Unseen to physical sight, the earth elementals, Devas and Angels are immemorial custodians of earth's growth; minerals, vegetables, forests, valleys and mountain strongholds possess their supervision.

Elemental creatures experience birth and death as do human beings, though their etheric forms sometimes exist for several centuries. It is these lives which ensoul the infinitesimal structures of nature, causing them to circulate the "breath of life" into its somnolent features. One of the most famous descriptions of a tree Deva is that of Frazier's "God of Aricia," found in his *Golden Bough*.

Legends of the water beings fill many volumes. Despite all man's primitive enlargements, we find sufficient repetitions in time-worn records to realize that nearly all primordial religions paid respect to the etheric inhabitants of the water kingdom. Dwelling in etheric bodies, undines, naiads, mermaids, nymphs and water sprites had for habitats lakes, streams, brooks, marshes, caves and oceans. It is difficult to understand the meaning of the sirens of the seas. It might be that sailors and adventurers were due to receive psychic testings, and their testers resembled warning sirens. Again, the legends about these water temptresses might have alluded to man's rationalization of his response to instinctive forces within himself.

The literature of our earliest ancestors mentions residents of the Fire Kingdom. A well-known example of fire genii is found in Arabian Nights tales wherein fire beings become slaves to a lamp and its owner's wishes.

In the worship of the Hindus, Chinese, Japanese Shintoists, Romans and Greeks, supersensitive presences governed man's entire existence. There were gods presiding over the air, dawn, fire, wind, home and household. Men felt protective spirits around them whenever they traveled. At home they were surrounded by their familiar spirits who guarded the land, provisions, and loved ones.

Minerva in Rome and Athena in Greece symbolized a high attainment of Angelhood. The Parthenon became a shrine to great presences, revealed by different names in these two rival countries.

Apollo, the mythical Greek god, more nearly resembles a description of an Angel Prince than do any other of the mythical deities. In the literature of Christianity and Islam, Apollo is analogous with the Archangel Michael. Of Apollo it was said, "Nothing false or impure might be brought near him; his was a cleansing and enlightening power."* As the most popular of Greek deities, Apollo was venerated for prophecy and healing gifts.

Grecian and Roman myths abound with mythical tales of beings whom they called *muses, gods or goddesses,* but upon whom the universal title, "Angel," would fit more suitably. Mythology becomes absorbingly interesting when we possess this key to its mysteries.

Another revered Roman goddess of Angelic origin was Vesta. This beneficent being was accorded rule over the fires of private and public buildings. In her honor a flame burned continuously in every home and shrine throughout Rome, signifying she belonged to the Fire Order. Priestesses consecrated to altar worship and service were honored "vestal virgins."

Greek and Roman Mythology by Jessie Tatlock; Century Co.

26

Vesta's duties included supervision of subordinate deities distinguished as Penates and Lares. Penates were regarded as more advanced than the Lares. The highest Penates directed the affairs and prosperity of the Roman Empire. Special Penates presided over towns and others were deemed guardians of stewardship in the home. Images of these supernatural guardians were placed in the central part of each home, called the *penetralia*. When the family moved, this foremost and most treasured image within the penetralia was carefully removed for installation in the new residence.

Lares, the equivalent of the spirits of the land in other countries, were fondly regarded by each family because they were believed to protect the health and happiness of the household. Romans welcomed and praised their faithful Penates and Lares, and through this inclusion of these familiar beings each home became a private temple. In Rome it became customary for every home to have a genius who inspired, healed and strengthened his charges in a way similar to the Christian's awareness of Guardian Angels. Only in China were gods accepted as closely and intimately by humans as in the Roman Empire.

Today we recognize in the Penates a group of National Angels of graded unfoldments and services. The Lares in Christian terminology would now receive the title, "Guardian Angel."

As they experience increased tensions in present-day living, many persons are searching for inward peace and an unmistakable contact with the Divine Presence. They will find few realities which can answer their inmost needs and stir them to nobler living as will the awareness of the actual nearness of Angelic Hosts.

27

Certain melodies are definitely related to celestial realms. A musical selection which was inspired by the chantings of those Angels who guard human beings is the *Children's Prayer* from the opera *Hansel and Gretel* by Humperdinck. Whenever this strain is presented through the opera, over radio symphonically, or by a recording, the *music* (not the words of the singers) ushers in the Angels, for it is their song. Whenever I have heard this inspiring tune I have always observed that thought forms resembling white camellias, fluttered into the auditorium or home where the music was enjoyed. These are the prayers of the Guardian Angels for their charges and for humanity.

The late Fedor Chaliapin's singing in a recording entitled *Credo* still attracts music elementals that flood the atmosphere with their multiformed undulations. His recorded bass voice has the power to attract Music Angels, and because of this his offerings are festivals of musical flares and jettings of harmonic power.

On sacred holidays we should try to hear Handel's *Hallelujah Chorus*. Whenever this music is sung, the Angels of the astral and mental worlds join the chorus and their accompaniment is a thousand times more joyous and victorious than the human parts. This is one musical number whose outpourings are turned completely toward the Lord Christ. The love, praise and devotion which radiates from this chorus to Him is said to be one of man's purest tributes for this Wayshower of our humanity.

Through the way of the arts have traveled many beings from celestial spheres. Too frequently these messengers become so bewildered by this planet's wayfaring, or so homesick for their homelands, that they forget nearly all of the messages they carry.

William Blake remains an enigma to those who try to fit him into the accepted pattern of human being. It is only when we recognize him as a "Bright Messenger" from shoreless spaces that we begin to comprehend his uniqueness. When still a boy, Blake saw Angels standing in a tree by a roadside. When adult, he saw the earth and air peopled with presences who were interested in man's destiny. This sensitive genius, whose religion was pantheistic, was an Angel of the Word, a creative Angel.

William Wordsworth was also a visitor from regions beyond. Although not as advanced a spirit as Blake, he retained sufficient higher dimensional senses to realize the nearness of invisible companions.

Another celestial harbinger was the gifted John Keats. When he left this world at twenty-five years of age, he had written as maturely and immemorably as those poets who lived to be aged. Before his death he told a friend, "The other day, during a lecture, there came a sunbeam into the room, and with it a whole troop of creatures floating in the ray; and I was off with them to Oberon and fairyland."

The bright messengers were familiar to Swedenborg. Once the mystic was believed to have undergone physical death. He was revived and later returned to consciousness. He shared with confidants the revelations he knew during his brief suspension from the body. Two Angels had conversed with him and told him valuable truths. They had not used vocal organs for speech, but had simply looked into his eyes and he had fathomed their thoughts.

29

For man's highest protection and surest inner development, he needs more than ever before to align himself in thought, love and reverence to the guardianship of Angels. To commune with them in prayer and meditation, his thoughts, acts and purposes need refining. Of one thing he can be certain—as he grows in spiritual consciousness, he shall be drawn more closely to the fellowship of Angelic Hosts.

In times of worship, crisis, or even during an enjoyment of nature's beauties, a few persons have known a sudden rapturous enlightenment of one of the most inspiring realities of the Eternal Creator. They have come into contact with the Kingdom of Angels, a path of God's evolving life well represented in the sacred writings of all great religions, and in the poetry and art of every advanced civilization.

We realize then that the Angelic Kingdom serves mankind faithfully and selflessly long before men become aware and appreciative of the shining ones, or useful to them. Perhaps a way by which we may become of humble use to Angelic Couriers is to strive to be *reverent, conscious conductors of ideas, means and powers* which originate in their realms. Angels can convey energy and Light to us in several ways, especially through nature, music and a spiritualized consciousness. All they desire from man is reverence for God, love which is inclusive, and an earnest questioning which contains sufficient courage to venture into boundaries beyond dogma and intellectual pharisaism into the clear light of awareness and realization.

THE OPEN DOOR OF NATURE

ALTHOUGH the path of nature beings is generally defined as belonging to the Angelic evolution, its youngest natives in the nature realm differ as greatly from a highly evolved Angel as an Australian bushman differs from a mature genius of the type of Albert Schweitzer. There are innumerable gradations of manifested progress in the human consciousness and the same order of growth pervades the vast Angelic evolution.

As one develops extended vision, nature acquaints him with the humblest as well as the grandest aspects of its kingdom. Then it is that we discern golden glints of truth within musty and antiquated myths. These shining facets free us from narrow and limiting concepts of God. New horizons greet us, divesting the landscape and the heavens of their veilings. We perceive sacred *life* in stones, trees, fields, rivers and clouds. Creation receives the attention of powers never profaned nor penetrated by folklore.

True understanding of the wonders within nature is revealed by Elizabeth Browning through her words:

Every common bush afire with God,

But only he who *sees* takes off his shoes.

A noteworthy revelation nature invariably shares with confidants is this: Everything which lives either possesses intelligence or is acted upon by intelligence. However humble each form of life may be on evolution's ladder (a vine, for example), it possesses the innate instinct to seek sunlight and will extend itself

31

through dark areas until sunlight is reached. This instinctive knowledge is a form of intelligence. Again, no one can look upon a many-faceted diamond with its flashing of many hues without marveling at the mind which created it.

The intelligence of nature discloses to seeking investigators that much in the physical realm receives impetus and development through directing intelligences from the superphysical side of existence. The trees we love, the very sweep of the terrain, the weather we sense, are all acted upon by higher-dimensional minds which work under unchangeable laws to keep the earth inhabited. In fact, all living things in nature are influenced by intelligences whose missions revolve around their physical and inward growth, development and awakenment. In admiration of the forms we behold, we want to remember to salute those God-commissioned beings who dwell on planes invisible to our physical perception. By saluting them and appreciating their ministrations, we shall draw into a closer bond of acquaintanceship with these busy servers.

Go to national parks, not alone to see the outer beauty that they hold, but also to sense the *inner presences* that guard and permeate these localities. You will gain much more from your pilgrimages by including a spiritual awareness of the loving minds that make the nature shrines places of peace.

Just as you find a different variety of trees, shrubs or flowers in various areas, so do you come in contact with nature beings whose appearance, emanation and service differ from range to range. Let your inner faculties of intuition and perception identify the invisible powers enveloping the places you visit. One forest will be surcharged with healing energies which are especially invigorating to the etheric body. Another mountain fastness will possess a strong current of reverence for God. Lake regions are usually attuned to radiations of peace. The open country quickens keenness of mind. These contrasting vibrations are largely due to the type of beings which ensoul the various territories.

Because Mt. Lassen in Northern California is a volcanic site, the nature spirits there are a strange combination of fire and earth beings. Zion National Park contains great stately Angels of Power, whereas, not many miles away, Bryce Canyon National Park is inhabited by presences which are particularly gentle and loving.

In the out-of-doors we discover Deva shrines, temples and playgrounds. Zion National Park is a Deva Cathedral radiating First Ray waves of spiritual power. Bryce Canyon as well as Yosemite and Yellowstone National Parks belong to the Deva playgrounds. Even they have their distinction, since Bryce is a Sixth Ray center; Yosemite, Third Ray; and Yellowstone, Fourth Ray. Human beings as well as Devas feel strongest kinship with nature temples or playgrounds on their own rays.

All of Mt. Rainier National Park forms a Nature Cathedral whose altar is graced by the presence of a very advanced Nature Being, known as the "Lord of the Mountain." He has attained this high rank in the Nature Kingdom through fidelity and service to the Highest. The temple vibrations issuing from His domain extend their beams into those communities and cities which are nearby on all sides of the mountain.

One of the lessons this sacred center discloses is that

the worship of God is natural in every kingdom. Even the builders of nature's forms are striving toward an attainment in consciousness and power which is exemplified to them in the Lord of Mt. Rainier.

Infinitely soul-stirring are unexpected glimpses of Angelic Orders at their work. Almost resolutely, I daily confine myself to labors at my desk, while outside, little builders are gaily gliding in and about our flower garden. Occasionally I steal to the windows of our study for a sight of those fairy beings, and the joy that swells up from within as I watch these tiny servers is both relaxing and refreshing.

At night, when we have taken our dogs and cats for a long walk in the foothills, we have found ourselves suddenly in the presence of glorious company. One evening a walk was lengthened so that I might observe a being of considerable size who proved to be a director of the Weather Angels. The communications between this Superior and His commands were lost to me, but, along with the Nature Devas, my higher sensibilities were quickened by this Great One's appearance.

It has been joyful, too, when near our cottage to see the silent, loving figure of the Angel of the Home. Her duties of renewing the etheric forces are usually performed when we are away from the home either in body or in spirit while asleep. There are many homes that have Angels protecting them. There are numerous individuals who, when they walk into the countryside, are companioned by pure presences. Our part is to greet them and to love them even though their forms are still invisible to our physical sight.

At Snoqualmie Falls in Washington state we have

observed a Water Guardian as tall as the height of the falls. Such beings are usually of tremendous size and are of very advanced unfoldment. The younger water elementals, who pass through the aura of such a being, gain a considerable surcharge of renewal.

It is interesting to watch what takes place in the superphysical aspect of the culture of flowers and growing things. While beautiful builders pour their energies into unfolding blossoms, others busy themselves with the tasks of opening leaves and stirring the flow of life energy through the plant and root system.

Imaginative accounts of the service of builders fill the story books of children. Fairy tales are often based upon verities of nature's actual superphysical activities. An example of informative tales of this kind is Kingsley's, *Water Babies.*

At Questhaven, overshadowing Inspiration Point, our highest peak, a person having clairvoyance would observe a Lieutenant Deva, a high Nature Spirit. He would witness nightly gatherings of nature presences in Mystic Mountain to the south. The advanced Tree Deva whose home is in the largest live oak tree would be discovered gliding from oak to oak; but at nightfall he would be found again in his own great tree. At all times of the day would the graceful sylphs of the air be seen above the chaparral, moving about like bees in their quest for honey. So, too, would be enjoyed the tiny, beautiful builders whose movements are perceived about both wild and cultivated flowers. Always at the major points of day—dawn, high noon, and sunset—would the Angels of the Sun be noticeable.

The colorful figure pictured in the frontispiece of this

volume is intended to represent an Angel of the Sun. This type of Angelic Server has reached a high degree of attainment and wields an invincible power which energizes the higher bodies of human beings.

Momentous are the occasions of dawn and sunset. We feel the earth standing reverent in these two high periods, and we then long to understand something of the inner experience of these hours.

As the curtain of our inner sight is lifted, a sunrise becomes an unforgettable event. Every dawn we thus witness contains even more beauty and more power than the one preceding it.

Before the break of sunlight, earthly and spiritual creatures busy themselves to be ready for that vibrant moment when the disc of the sun shines on them as it rises above the horizon.

The Solar Logos (the Sun) is the most advanced initiate of our whole solar system. He is a Being whose spiritual energy is many times more effective than His outer radiations of heat and light. His will ordains the laws of our universe. His glorious beauty and purity of consciousness is more luminous than His visible fiery body.

The first man dimly realized that after the Supreme Invisible Spirit, this Presence in the sun merited his veneration. The myths and legends relating to the Sun God honor an actual Being who has been the source of our physical light and life since mankind's inception.

Were we to be affected by the spiritual vibrations of the Solar Logos as strongly as we are by His physical energy, we should be shattered by the power. There are two reasons why we do not receive these full chargings.

36

First, the earth's highest Initiate sends us only a portion of His emanations (the majority of His inner power is broadcast into the interstellar spaces between the planets). Second, the Angels of the Morning add to the sun's radiations their broadcasts of music and healing currents which they are uniquely able to transmit.

We sense the activities of the Angels of the Morning even before we see the sun rise. They always precede the progress of the sun's rays over the earth's surface. Their ministrations cause a quickening of our love and thanksgiving.

In this planet's pilgrimage through the firmaments the hour of high noon is the cardinal occasion of the day. At this time the Logos of our Star attains a position wherein He can most effectively charge those bodies and beings which are in line with the direct reception of His rays. It is the supreme moment when He can send out greater spiritual and physical forces to every living thing—the moment when no guards are necessary for the shielding of His rays.

High noon is the only period of the day when there are no hosts standing between the fiery orb and ourselves. This strong radiation of energy continues for about thirty minutes. After that time the Sun Beings again form a veil between the luminary and those bodies His Light shines upon.

Viewed from the inner planes, the Logos' dispersion of Light causes the etheric world to glow with saffron luminescent beams, whereas in the astral world His radiations are a lucid larkspur blue. The variations of color tones are meaningful. Beings from the nature kingdom who work upon the etheric levels require the rhythmic stimulation of the Logos, and His force reaches them as a flame-colored wave of shimmering Light. This charging serves both as an internal purification and a stimulant. It acts upon the accumulated etheric matter which fills the auras of the builders and absorbs this substance.

The noontide rays bear irresistible influence upon our own etheric bodies. We sense it as a glowing of this delicate body, and we are even aware of an afterglow for an indefinite period. These sensations are most perceptible when we are in the sunlight of the outdoors. For the keenness that it brings to our outer and inner bodies, sun bathing is, indeed, a reliable elixir. Everyone should take advantage of the sun rays every available day, preferably at the high noon hour.

In the astral world, sunlight is never-fading though its blue current of healing is revitalized periodically. It is this soft-tinted aureole in the "atmosphere" of this dimension which makes harmony and relaxation natural to everyone. Every time we are in the outdoors and receive the direct beams of the sun, our astral bodies are cleansed of certain negative accumulations and we breathe more freely, inwardly, because of this release.

Although both the Angels of the Morning and the Angels of the Evening serve the Planetary Logos, they are different types of beings performing different services.

At morning the etheric world teems with activity in preparation for the dawn. Then follows a hush of adoration as the sun triumphantly beams over the horizon, after which nature and men are joyously ensouled with stimulus for activities of the day.

Few of us greet the sunrise, but when we do, let us

remember the Logos who makes possible our life on earth, and His Hosts, among them the Angels of the Morning and Evening. Knowledge of Him and those orders devoted to Him should accelerate our reception of His influence. In the out-of-doors we are enveloped by radiant energies set in motion by Devanic activity. Sunrise and sunset periods contain energies that flow from Angels of the Dawn and Evening into the aura of the planet. From sunrise we receive tides of renewal whose inner incentive is toward rededication. At evening, outgoing energy tides turn us toward peaceful reflections upon the day. One seer who observed the ministry of Angel Presences said, "At eventide they will examine thee." That is somewhat the inner impression we gather at twilight as we observe a sunset. We sense that we are being studied by powers whose estimate of us will be recorded upon the tablets of our own development.

At twilight, human beings and nature spirits reluctantly observe the sun's setting. This should be proof of our strong dependence upon the sun! When its rays brighten our day everyone's disposition is happily affected. How frequently we find tendencies toward anxiety or irritation on cloudy or stormy days!

Angels of the Morning are the sun's vanguard. Angels of the Evening are its rear guard. Every host has a specific work. Each is unknowingly acknowledged by every nature devotee. Most of us sense that something wonderful is inwardly happening around us when the sky is a garden of emblazoned colors. Intuition acquaints us with a true mystical nature ritual. Regardless of the physical appearances of sunset, on the etheric level of existence (as well as on the higher planes) sunset is always a spectacle of splendor. However, when we are fortunate enough to witness a glorious afterglow of beauty upon the physical level we should be able to discern increased power vibrating to earth from the heavens.

How evening stars draw one to reflection and thanksgiving! We understand why the ancients believed that "the heavens *declare* the glory of God." Maimonides stated that the globes (planets) are the bodies of living and rational beings, and that they serve their God and praise and glorify Him "with great praise and mighty glorification. *Through the oath the stars complete their course and He calls them by their names, and they answer Him from eternity to eternity.*"

Usually at sundown the color *orange* predominates. This is meaningful for on the inner levels it is this tone which steals into our atmosphere from the mingled benediction of the Angels of the Evening. Orange in our sky, and invisibly in the ethers around us, *is a blessing for courage* which this host broadcasts. The message which these benefactors chant is summed up in these words:

"Until the sun again strengthens you, have courage.
Be fearless, for the night comes to bring you peace,
reflection, and rest.
As you acted in faith, so shall you rest in peace."

As these Deva chants are sung, the etheric envelope of the earth is charged with this auric shade of encouragement.

Have you ever stood in a mountain fastness long after sundown with only the stars overhead? Except for the calls of night birds and animals, the earth was asleep. Like a gentle scarf, night covered everything with repose.

Man and nature spirits strive best in the sunlight hours. Day is the time for effort. Night is the time of assimilation and reception. At nightfall the body consciousness wearies and finds rest in sleep. Our inner consciousness, however, disengages itself from the drowsing body to follow the call of the Spirit into regions of beauty and places of power.

Were we to step into the etheric kingdom we should pass many great Angels of the Night whose Light is especially luminous around their faces as though they held candles to see by. This order is one of the most gentle and loving that touches the life of man and young nature spirits, but their duties sometimes necessitate their use of more brilliant Light than most Angels wield. In a sense, the Angels of the Night are policing the etheric regions and the lower astral, for it is in these dimensions that elemental forms and lowly evolved beings wander. Ordinarily these lives are harmless, but when aroused through man's profanity and lust, a few of these creatures could become dangerous. There are rare cases of genuine obsession. When they do occur, man's evil action has attracted them.

The watching Angels of the Night greet those human beings who consciously (or unknowingly) take leave of their physical bodies. To meet one of these pure watchers is like being touched by a fragrant breeze. Their purity, love, and deep spirituality is stabilizing to lesser souls. Many times these Angels act as directors and informants to those who need direction.

Those who are unfortunate enough to leave the physical plane through suicide or accident are received by this order. Never was anyone more lovingly ministered to than these untimely arrivers.

It is at night that most of the nature world has its conclaves and initiations. Those who are nature spirits work so intently, even though they may serve in groups, that there is little or no association with others during the sunlit hours of activity. It is different, however, in the evening, for worship, instruction and progress is made in unity (of a kind we would not yet understand). The reverse is true of man. He has relationships with his fellowmen during the day hours. At night, he becomes a lone searcher.

Among the Weather Angels, there are two types we should especially respect—they are Angels of Force, and Angels of Calm. The first group has charge of winds, storms and all manner of turbulent conditions. The second group controls the elements that induce fair, sunny weather. One day in the mountains, mist rolled past our camp, moistening the whole forest. Soon a high wind started and later everything seemed tumultuous. A heavy storm was brewing. I saw the strange Power Beings who are so dynamic one can scarcely observe them without shuddering. They are God's workers, too, but I think of them with awe, because of the upheavals they often cause.

That night I prayed that the Angels of Calm hover near our camp. Within a few hours, all was peaceful and quiet about us. Yet, the next day we learned at the post office that it had rained the night before in our vicinity. My husband and I exchanged significant glances, and together sent out a prayer of gratitude for the shelter given us.

Wind Angels serve in the nature kingdom working with weather conditions to bring productivity to the earth. The Angels of Wind and Angels of Calm serve together to regulate the weather and bring changes to certain areas.

Human beings are permitted to ask for their blessing or protection whenever they require it. A young man was crossing a mountain pass, pulling a house trailer behind his automobile, when the wind became so strong and violent that he feared it would overturn his light car and send him over the embankment. He stopped and reverently sent forth a prayer that the Angels of Calm come near to protect him from the gale as he crossed the mountain. No sooner had he opened his eyes, than he noted a lessening in the force of the wind. He continued his journey without further difficulty. His gratitude for this expression of protection from the nature realm was sincere and lasting.

All about us exist the wonders of nature, yet how much wider, deeper and more reverent becomes our appreciation when we admit the inner side of our outer existence. Go to the hills, mountains, canyons, desert or seashore and there you will find intelligent healers and teachers!

Although nature spirits and Angels are not directly associated with man, they serve him through their stirring of nature to its rhythmic unfoldment. For this service we are dependent upon nature spirits and we should be filled with gratitude for their manifold ministries. Yet, the chief blessing of realization concerning their inner existence is the inspiration they arouse in us through their selflessness, impersonality, beauty and devotion.

Nature tells us that we can learn more of God by observing Him through His handiwork. She promises to initiate us into the wonders of life *after* we appreciate life around us *everywhere*—after our veneration for the Supreme Spirit includes the visible *and* invisible regions of being. She speaks to us in realizations of this kind, "Look about you and profit by all you see. Whatever of good you find represented, you can become. Your thoughts can be as crystalline as the flowing stream. Your character can be as strong as yonder stalwart pine. The light of day and the peace of night can likewise radiate from your heart. Bless everything you behold and be prepared to receive my pictorial or symbolical messages."

I HEARD THE MOUNTAIN SINGING

Did a voice call?
Pushing the shutter back
I leaned against the storm,
Saw the eerie dawn-light sifting
Through the snow.

               No sound save the wind
Swishing the flakes in arcs of white
Intangible as breath.

                    I waited—
Quiet as the quiet trees,
There was a portent in the hour;

THE OPEN DOOR OF NATURE

This time, this place, bordered eternity's edge,
Immortal threshold!
Then . . . riding the highest wind it came——
A note of music . . .

                Then others
In thin sweet dissonance,
Unearthly tones, elusive . . .
Harp-like chords . . . faint . . . far away . . .
I heard the mountain singing!

            —Marietta Conway Kennard

Tacoma News Tribune, April 17, 1948

45

ANGELIC ORDERS SERVING THE CHRIST

"For by Him were all things created that are in
heaven, and that are in earth, visible and invisible,
whether they be thrones, or dominions, or principalities, or powers: all things were created by Him,
and for Him; and He is before all things, and by
Him all things consist."—*Colossians* 1:16-17

A STUDY of the Holy Trinity is incomplete without
a consideration of the hosts who serve that Trinity. These powers aid and influence us on the spiritual
planes of being, for theirs is the effort of attuning us
ever more closely as a humanity to the Triune Spirit.

There are far more variations of Angelic life than
there are human distinctions. Everyone in this kingdom
from the most minute to the greatest form *is intent upon
serving God.* Daniel had a vision in which he beheld
their constant endeavor: "A swift stream of fire issued
forth from before Him: thousands upon thousands
ministered to Him and ten thousand times a hundred
thousand stood before Him."—*Daniel* 7:10

Mankind is self-indulgent and most forgetful of the
source from which it originated, but the shining ones
of even the lowest orders are continually intent upon
praising and glorifying God. Greater association with
the Angels lifts our minds from ourselves and focuses
them upon ways and means by which we too may assist
in establishing God's Plan.

What inconceivable wonders encircle us in the higher
dimensions of existence! Multitudes sing hosannas to
the Pristine Spirit unendingly, while legions of pure

beings are active in carrying the will of God into every plane of manifestation. Man alone is deaf and blind to the inner glories around him, because his consciousness is still too enslaved by his physical senses.

Our human consciousness is broadened as we consider the existence of lives utterly unlike us in nature, but one with us in service to the Highest. Though we have not realized it, much of the good we know, such as the loveliness of nature on the outer plane, and spiritual protection on the inner planes, is the work of bright, superior beings. We are aware of the boundless blessings that come to us from initiates on our human path of unfoldment, yet by turning our attention more truly inward we become appreciative of the myriad benefactors who are silently active around us.

To some, the revelations of the higher orders might seem to make their studies of reality rather complex. They would wish to learn how to place these unfoldments within the range of their daily consciousness.

Analogy offers the best means of our understanding the normal relation between our unfoldment and their ever-present nearness. Because each of us has a certain pilgrimage of growth to achieve, we may compare ourselves to a traveler headed toward a specific destination. Our goal is spiritual unfoldment of an ever-widening experience. Throughout our travels in this lifetime we must hold one-pointedly to the course that leads us safely to our journey's end. This specificness concerning self-discipline and the attainment of our inherent spiritual powers is the pathway that leads to our intended destination—spiritual maturity.

Yet, as we journey through the passing of days, we

need not be so self-absorbed that we fail to observe the beauties of the scenes (or experiences) that we pass. We can still travel in a straight course and yet enjoy the wonders that form the scenery of our progress. How impressive and expansive to the frontiers of our contemplation are the cloud-etched skies and the mysteries of the stars at night! We continue our footsteps toward our goal even while we recognize that there is more of life than just ourselves and our charted pathway.

One of the most serious hindrances of our Soul's progress is the *pride* human beings feel in their own self-esteem. A great mind, endowments of skill or leadership can close us to the surrounding glories, and restrict not only our sight but our feeling for the numberless Godly-created forms around us.

There are persons who believe themselves spiritual who are bound in the mire of their exaggerated opinion of the greatness of human beings. Time and humility will free them from their self-imposed bondage to limited ideas.

Certainly, man has the Light of God within him; but so have countless numbers of orders whose expressions of Godliness are so much more radiant and steady than our own. It gives us strength to realize that those above us, far from being proud of their attainments, are desirous of raising us gently into those higher estates of mind in which we *know* we form a *part* of a great plan that is being unfolded in every octave of existence.

Especially by Angels is God's Will done, as is clear in our Lord's Prayer: ". . . Thy Will be done in earth *as it is in heaven.*"

One of the foremost needs in spiritual studies is an

overcoming of the vague acceptance we have accorded the reality of Angels, for their actual nearness is too great and wondrous for superficial assent. Those who are earnest shall emerge from dim conceptions of this resplendent truth as finer, wiser, and more blessed Christians, because one more veil shall have been parted for their deeper penetration.

Truth knows endless rebirth. When reality becomes distorted or veiled by man-made concepts, it will seek re-embodiment again at a later period. *What is really true is true always.* Thus nothing of vital significance can be denied men forever since if certain truths are withheld from them in one life they shall be recovered in subsequent lifetimes.

So it is in relation to the existence of splendid superphysical orders of being. Knowledge concerning Angelic Hosts may have been kept from man for hundreds of years but truth itself will be reborn and liberated at last from the tyranny of suppression and ignorance.

The Angelic Kingdom consists of God-created beings who, like mankind, press toward the goal of perfection and ultimate union with the Supreme Spirit. Angels are purer than man, their very spirituality equipping them to be mediators between heaven and earth.

Angelic consciousness functions "vertically," it is said, whereas human beings seem to view life "horizontally." Angels have a conscious attunement with octaves of life far above them in development as well as with younger Devanic forms below their own levels. Man often finds it difficult to love both those who are above him in evolution and sub-human life, but with illumination man achieves the "vertical" consciousness after which he realizes a oneness with all levels of aspiring creatures. It is then that he glimpses something of the inclusive good-will which is radiated so vibrantly by all within the Angelic Kingdom. Even the lowest orders of Angels are higher than uninitiated man. For that reason the Psalmist observed, "He hath given His Angels charge over thee, to keep thee in all thy ways."—*Psalm* 91:11

Since the Divine Will has decreed that Angels be the custodians of man, their importance to us in our development deserves sincere consideration. Of our own spiritual instruction and direction toward attainment, God explains: "Behold, I send an Angel before thee, to keep thee in the way, and to bring thee into the place which I have prepared."—*Exodus* 23:20

Our association with Angelic Orders comes chiefly through appreciative contact with nature and with the planetary work of the Christ Spirit. As Christ Hierarch and World Teacher, the Lord Jesus needs not only the assistance of perfected human beings but likewise the helpfulness of the Angelic Couriers. Masters busy themselves with specific labors for mankind. Their communication with us is through Light paths which they maintain. Angelic ministrants are occupied with the work of cleansing, quickening and inspiring mankind from superphysical levels. They create great "clouds" of force which envelop this globe, particularly noticeable at sacred festivals.

Their access to human affairs is best and most direct at Christmas, Easter and on Sundays. During these rhythmic occasions the superphysical currents about the earth are intensified, while the entire globe is aligned to a new and vibrant keynote. No wonder the veil grows very transparent during these events of outpouring so that the very earth is permeated by Angelic frequencies. It was to such occasions that Wordsworth alluded when he wrote:

The earth and the common face of nature
Spake memorable things.

Every day we can do a great deal for the spiritualizing, refining, beautifying and the safefolding of our own home by placing around it a ring-pass-not of the White Light of the Christ. We should also pray to be worthy of attracting an Angel who will ensoul the entire place with spiritual power. After a certain level of gratitude, idealization and good stewardship is reached, a Presence, known as the Spirit of the Home, reveals its mantling. From then on, the place seems infinitely dearer and has more Light within and about it.

To maintain a spiritual atmosphere, genuine love and harmony are necessary. In addition, we need to respect inward and outward cleanliness and order. Untidiness, like discords in music, emanates destructive forces. One who rightly evaluates the blessings of a home follows Jesus' rule, "Into whatsoever house ye enter, first say, 'Peace be to this house.' "—*Luke* 10:5

Our link with the Hierarchies of Spiritual Entities stretching endlessly above us is strengthened by frequent remembrance of them, especially on nature walks taken in awareness of the surrounding nearness of these great ones. At such times we should include a reflection upon the Recording Angels, with whom the Angels of Birth and Death serve. Since all our thoughts and aspirations are noted, we come within the attention of this order regularly. The Recording Angels organize our material of experience gathered in each incarnation. They guard the Akashic Records, storehouse of earth's unfading memories. When we make important decisions—when we fail or succeed—we are within the watchfulness of those whose ministry is to gather and make permanent our record of earth experience.

My husband and I with two understanding friends visited the Lincoln Memorial in Washington D.C. It is an imposing edifice, but what impressed me so deeply was what the tribute symbolized. The design of the memorial is a symbol of an initiate who works along the lines of humanitarian service.

The line of power issuing from the Inner Government of the World does not enshroud the Capitol building nor the stately White House, but instead, the Lincoln Memorial.

Above this edifice was a huge National Angel whose duty was to direct the force from the Master of America to those buildings, meetings or persons who required it. Enveloping the statue of Abraham Lincoln was another Great Angel who blessed each individual who looked upon the figure of this initiate.

A pathway of color transformed the aura of the place. A light orange, significant of courage, was radiant everywhere. This beam of color gradually faded beyond my seeing, into the vast heights of the higher dimensions.

To us, Lincoln Memorial was a symbol of tribute, expressing the regard and appreciation of our world toward a benefactor. Surely the architectural lines of the dedication were inspired by the Masters. To them, *all efforts,* consistently and loyally performed, proclaim a server.

Several years ago a member of my family brought a little black bulldog home, whom I called *Sambo*. Our little visitor's owner could not be found. No one advertised or called for him. To one of my lectures came a young woman, saddened by the recent death of her pet. I mentioned Sambo to her and her face beamed. That very day we took the little wanderer to his next mistress. His nature was extremely friendly, so he liked his new guardian at once. As we drove away, the young woman and Sambo watched our departure. Sambo, who had grown accustomed to me, appeared slightly perplexed and hurt at my leaving him. He seemed so uncertain as to whom he belonged, or where he was supposed to go. A pull on the leash immediately brightened his expression, for he was thus reminded that there was one who would direct him. Something about the little dog's bravery and trust touched me deeply. He made the best of circumstances, so easily and happily. The most impressive sight occurred just as we drove away. Looking back at the two on the sidewalk, I saw an Angel above my friends and immediately I recognized that even the great ones were sympathetic about the loneliness of a sad young woman and a little tramp dog.

In the whole Angelic Kingdom, from the youngest to the most exalted server, there is wholehearted endeavor and constancy of service. Every Angel contributes with fullest ardor to the fulfillment of this planet's goal.

Since we are ever within the observation and helpfulness of Angelic Hosts we should avail ourselves of some instruction regarding their natures and activities. Numberless orders and octaves of Angelic Beings fill the aura of our planet. Some of these shining hosts work directly under the Lord Jesus. Some are responsible to Angelic Directors who are endeavoring to lift the existence of animals on earth above neglect, abuse and pain.

We find that Angels are immortal, free of births and deaths to which human beings are subject. These holy messengers possess vivid beauty, energy which is electric, and a joyousness of nature that exceeds anything mortals ordinarily experience. Another quality which distinguishes them from all other creations is their keen sense of selfless service. Whatever is done is performed for love of helping, and the humblest creature is attended with the same patience and love that is shown the most evolved man. Every phase of their work is always carried out with thoroughness; no detail or circumstance is ever slighted.

BIBLICAL REFERENCES TO ANGELS

ALL churches and denominations composing Christianity should seek a better understanding of this glorious subject because so much concerning the inhabitants of higher worlds is hinted at in the Bible. In nearly half of the sixty-six books of our modern Bible, Angels are mentioned.

We shall look at just a few of these accounts to reveal how fully the companionship and instruction of Angels was accepted. In the sixteenth chapter of Genesis, Hagar is advised by one of God's Messengers. In her dilemma as to whether or not to flee from the home of Sarai and Abram, she is directed to return to her mistress. She obeys the Angelic prompting and her son, Ishmael, is born, who is generally conceded to be the forebear of the Arabic peoples.

In the second chapter of Judges we note, an Angel of the Lord came up to Bochim and said to the leaders of the children of Israel: "I have brought you unto the land which I sware unto your fathers; and I said, I will never break my covenant with you."

The stalwart prophet and judge, Gideon, said in awe-stricken tone, "I have seen an Angel of the Lord face to face."—*Judges* 6:22. This visitation came at a time when Gideon as leader needed and received wisdom in guiding his homeless people, the Israelites.

A heavenly one encouraged Elijah time and again, stabilizing his faith, with the result that his needs were always supplied whether simply meal and oil, (*I Kings*

17) or protection from untimely death at the hands of Queen Jezebel.—*I Kings* 19

Of exquisite beauty and deep truth is the incident of Elisha and his unseen helpers, after Elijah's "mantle of responsibility" has descended upon him. Beset on every hand by opposing factions, he and his faithful servant are hemmed in by warlike tribes. In dismay the young servant implores Elisha, "Alas, my master! *how shall we do?*" And Elisha answered, "Fear not: for they that be with us are more than they that be with the enemy." Then Elisha prayed, "Lord, I pray thee, open his eyes, that he may see." And the Lord opened the eyes (inner vision) of the young man: and he saw . . . behold. the mountain was full of horses and chariots of fire (conveyors of force) round about Elisha."—*II Kings* 6:15-17

Ornan (or Araunah) was counseled by a similar visitor in *I Chronicles* 21. Because of his gift of insight, Ornan "saw the Angel" who inspired David during troubled times to erect an altar of worship unto the Lord on the threshing floor of Ornan's peaceful land.

The high priest Zacharias heard prophetic news from the Archangel Gabriel (*Luke* 1) that he and his wife Elizabeth were to have a son, John the Baptist, the forerunner of the Messiah.

How well-known, in the same chapter, is the Archangel Gabriel's visit to Mary, the mother of our Lord! The earthly life of Jesus of Nazareth was companioned by unseen friends from birth through the ordeal of the cross. In the fourth chapter of Matthew is an account of the Angels who came to minister to our Lord after He had passed a severe test, a temptation, that marked an initiation. His great friends were there, too, the morning of His resurrection, to roll away the stone that barred the tomb.

Later, Angelic freers released Peter, Paul and Silas from prison. Philip was told the course he should travel by a shining one. It was an Angel who revealed to Cornelius where his servants would find Peter.

In the Book of Revelation, gradations of Angelic ranks and initiations are described by John. Three main classifications in the evolution of the Angelic Kingdom are:

1. The Cloud of Silent Witnesses before the Throne —Seraphim, Cherubim and Thrones.
2. The Advanced Orders—Dominions, Principalities, Powers, Virtues.
3. The Ranks of the Angels—Archangels, Angel Princes, all the Angels of specialized service and worship.

Let us review a portion of the work of each of these groups of servers:

The Seraphim, fervent, Divine Love ensouled beings, are synonymous with the fire of holy enthusiasm. This first seraphic host dedicates its invocations to the Eternal Creator's glory. The most highly developed beings are able to convey to us only a symbol of themselves. Thus it is that in literature and paintings we find the presence of Seraphim symbolically denoted by a young face with six wings on either side.

These adoring ones, who immediately surround the Most High Eternal One, steadfastly contemplate in love His ineffable glory—hence their name, *Seraphs,* coming from the Hebrew root meaning "love," in the sense of love being a consuming flame of pure adoration. It is from their supernal level that the Seraphim sound the highest notes in unison with the vast throngs whose praises form the "music of the spheres." Whenever we feel the need of expressing more fervent love for God in our devotions, a remembrance of the unceasing ardor of the Seraphim will help to strengthen our own adoration.

The Cherubim, about whom artists have only given us symbols, contemplate the Wisdom of God and *emanate that Wisdom.* They intone the Spirit of Truth as It mantles the earth's entire endeavor so that every living being will stir toward renewed growth.

Often the Cherubim are pictured as beautiful faces with four wings on each side covered with eyes. This denotes the full degree they have attained unto knowledge of God. A portion of their work consists of supporting the Comforter's (the Spirit of Truth) mission. In our thoughts concerning the Holy Comforter we should now add the realization that Cherubim are giving their powers to the mission of the third aspect of the Trinity, the Spirit of Truth.

Thrones administer the Divine Judgments of the Supreme Spirit. They create, as it were, the judiciary body of the highest orders. They imbue their executive duties with special consecration and instruct Dominions how to regulate and distribute their plans. In art, the Thrones are sometimes symbolized as winged heels that are full of eyes. The Thrones form a powerful spiritual *attraction* which will eventually lead every pilgrim, *in every kingdom,* back to his one nativity—unity with the Eternal Spirit.

Dominions are actually administrators of the will

58

of the Thrones, and are frequently signified by a flashing sword. Plans and orders for the unfoldment of manifested life originate first in the realm of the Dominions.

Virtues are beings capable of great spiritual integrity and activity. The early Christians believed that grace and miracles came under the jurisdiction of these lofty intelligences. Flashing armor is sometimes pictured to portray the Virtues. That which is ordained by the Dominions is executed by the Virtues. Meditation upon the patient, tireless functions of the Virtues should instill us with the will to persevere in our human accomplishments. Angels of Prayer work under the counsel and strengthening of this vast host, and will eventually enter the ranks of the Virtues.

Powers regulate the activities of spiritual purposes in such a way that confusion and opposition is overcome. They attack evil and encircle God's Plans (revealed by the Thrones) with their mighty pinions of Light.

Gregory believed that the Powers had charge of checking contrary forces; perhaps that is why they are represented by flashes of lightning in medieval art. The Powers guide the laws of cause and effect. Under these superiors do the Angels of Birth and of Death carry out the justice of God *on every plane.* The Archangel Michael and His hosts come under this order's supervision. In Wagner's opera, *Die Walkure,* the Battle Maid Brunhilde would be a representative of this type of Angel.

Principalities wield authority over human nations, governments, kings, leaders and world servers. They empower nations to carry out the Divine Pattern with which each nation is individually vested. They do not guard nor direct the policies of a nation, only its humanitarian incentives and its unique culture. The guardians of great movements, races and nations are known as Principalities. Great Angels in charge of various religions and national Angels are of this order. The Roman Penates would have served this holy group.

Archangels in all the holy books of the world are equally respected as being highly advanced emissaries intent on fulfilling missions entrusted to them by their Creator-God. They continually receive endowments of supernal energy with which to execute their tasks. Archangels possess tremendous development and could be in the ranks of any of the described Advanced Orders, but they choose to be interpreters between the higher orders and the Ranks of Angels and men. Thus Archangels are at the head of the Ranks of Angels.

The most familiar Archangels in sacred literature are Michael, Gabriel, Raphael and Uriel. *St. Michael*, a representative of the Powers, is particularly consecrated to cleansing persons, groups or localities of discord and evil. He is frequently revealed as a soldierly figure flashing a fiery sword. In some instances he is visioned as a Being clad in white holding a pair of scales. He is constantly attacking evil and challenging those engaged in wrongdoing to convert their motives and energies into God-directed channels. St. Christopher is another advanced soul whose efforts for humans would come within the guardianship of the Powers.

One of the most complete accounts of the Archangel Michael's earth missions is found in the little-known Apocryphal *Testament of Abraham.* * It deals with that

*by G. H. Box of University of London; Macmillan Co.

noble patriarch's unwillingness to leave the earth until he has experienced the mysteries of life and death. With Michael as his guide, they view evolving life on its many different planes, including the higher, heavenly realms of being.

The Archangel Gabriel is usually portrayed as carrying a lily, an olive branch, or a torch—each symbolical of the work he serves. Sacred literature has shown him announcing major duties or spiritual commissions to qualified earth-dwellers such as the Master Mary, Zoroaster, and Mohammed, as well as numerous others to be used as channels in the Divine Plan. Sacred books emphasize this Great Being's faithful service to mankind.

The Archangel Raphael is an appointed treasurer of creative talents to be entrusted to the worthy whose work will be to reveal beauty through the arts. In addition, this Great One has often been identified with healing missions as is cited in the fascinating story of Tobit.* Tobit, a worthy and devout man, is afflicted with blindness and eventual poverty. His greatest concern is naturally for his wife and son, Tobias. Tobit, whose upright life merits answer to his earnest prayer, is healed by the wise and timely ministrations of the Archangel Raphael in the guise of an unknown stranger. "And Raphael was sent to heal them both, that is, to scale away the whiteness of Tobit's eyes, and to give Sara for a wife to Tobias."—*Tobit* 3:17

In connection with this account of the "stranger" who brings about the meeting in a perfectly logical manner of Sara and Tobias, we recall the story of *The*

*The Apocrypha, Oxford University Press, London

Bishop's Wife, by Robert Nathan, wherein Angelic intervention and visitation is similarly illustrated. The Angel, "Dudley," works a transformation in every character his life touches. Appearing as an ordinary man, often this type of work is assumed by an Angel of Mercy who actually dons physical resemblance in order to cleanse the hearts and clarify the minds of men regarding eternal values.

The Archangel Raphael also wields healing currents and initiates the Healing Angels in the use of curative rays. He does not work with individuals but He directs spiritual beams into hospitals, institutions and homes where His healing beams are needed. The pilgrim's staff, a lyre, or hands outstretched in healing signify the blessing of the Archangel Raphael.

The Archangel Uriel is the alchemist imparting transforming ideas to those who, when ill, discouraged or unsuccessful, need to realize how to achieve their goals constructively with renewed dedication.

Such an instance of Divine help is found in the Apocryphal *Second Book of Esdras.** Esdras, a God-loving Israelite, is much concerned over the state of his homeless countrymen. He is enlightened by lengthy and intimate communion with One who identifies Himself as Uriel. Esdras thereupon records the profound wisdom imparted by the Archangel on cosmic, eternal truths. An insight into the *obedience* and true humility born of intelligence, that marks these Great Ones, is apparent in the reply Uriel makes to Esdras' very human question: "How and when shall these things come to pass? May I live until that time? What shall happen in those future

*The Apocrypha, Oxford University Press, London

days of earth's destiny?" And unto these things Uriel, the Archangel, answered: "I may tell thee of the main part: but as touching thy life, *I am not sent to shew thee; for I do not know it."*—Esdras 4

Uriel is also associated with the arts, particularly music. Noteworthy mention is made of the Archangel Uriel in traditional accounts as being the instructor of the World Teacher, Rama, 10,000 B.C. With what long and patient service He has blessed humanity!

To be an Angel of lesser or higher rank signifies a being who has achieved enlightenment and who is thenceforth capable of disseminating the Light of God into all the regions and among all the lives God has created at levels less evolved than his own. The multiple divisions of the labors of Angels are too numerous to mention, much of it pertaining to superphysical activities to which man is not related.

In the realms of Angel Servers are innumerable ministers, among them the Angels of Birth and the Angels of Death. At death we confront those Angels who have charge of severing the silver cord. These beings are highly advanced, of the Order of the Powers. Their compassion and gentleness imbues the human soul with confidence and a willingness to pursue the trails of higher dimensions. For a long period (long only in earth years) the human soul who has witnessed the fourth and fifth dimensional existence remains in a contemplative state. He gradually begins to sense that he must return to the outer, three-dimensional world until he has conquered it. Because of this, plans for one's next life are slowly and carefully evolved. During this passive stage a human being is receptive to suggestions from superior beings whom he may not even discern in his indrawn condition. Then Karmic Angels direct the planned outlines of the coming life. As already stated, the superiors known as the Powers who guide the laws of cause and effect (karma) carry out, with justice, God's immutable laws. They appoint to these Angelic Servers magnificent tasks which only compassionate and God-filled beings are equipped to perform with perfection.

Guardian Angels—The Angels with whom we are most likely to be in contact, whether we are aware of them or not, are Guardian Angels. Every human being is under the watchfulness of some group of guardian beings, but it is not until man yearns for spiritual growth that he attracts the sponsorship and help of a single Guardian Angel.

The role of the Guardian Angel is illustrated by Jesus in *Matthew* 18:10 when He says of children: "Take heed that ye despise not one of these little ones; for I say unto you, that in heaven *their Angels* behold the face of my Father which is in heaven."

This being, who is always feminine in polarity, becomes the aspirant's teacher and minor initiator through many ordeals while spiritual maturity is being achieved. For man's highest protection and surest inner development he needs more than ever to align himself in love, thought and reverence to the guardianship of Angels. To coummune with them, one's thoughts, acts and purposes need refining. Of one thing the aspirant can be certain: as he grows in spiritual consciousness he shall be drawn more closely into fellowship with Angelic Hosts.

During religious services when groups have gathered for reverent worship, Religious Angels are present and are in constant motion. Thought waves from individuals ray out—waves created by hymns, prayers, meditations and rituals. The Religious Angels dip into these waves and focus strong spiritual radiations upon persons in need of special assistance. Every sincere group that mentions God is like a signal-fire, attracting Angels who serve to strengthen the bond of communion between God and aspiring human channels.

We shall not become confused if we remember the oft-spoken truths: that whatever help we receive is of God, whether administered by Angels or man; and that while humanity is prone to become "worshipers of idols," it is possible for us to have knowledge of the reality of Angels and at the same time realize it is to the Divine God Presence that we must render our *first* reverence, love and devotion. It is needful that we be aware of the pure hosts encircling us, that, by respect for them and their offices, we may increase the recognition of God's extensive waves of life.

When we make Truth our lifelong quest, it shall become for us an ever-expanding illumination through which we perceive the throbbing endlessness of God. If we are intelligently receptive, then Divine Realities shall ever be creative inlets within our minds into which the ocean of truth shall flow with renewing and enlarging calm.

"Everlasting God, who hast ordained and constituted the services of Angels and men in a wonderful order, mercifully grant that as Thy Holy Angels always do Thee service in heaven, so by Thy appointment they

65

may succor and defend us on earth, through Jesus Christ our Lord."—*From a Church Litany.*

REFERENCE LIST

Genesis—16:7, 9, 10, 11; 19:1, 15; 28:12; 32:1.
Numbers—20:16.
Judges—2:1, 4.
I Kings—19:5.
II Kings—6:15, 16, 17.
I Chronicles—21:12, 15, 16, 18, 20, 27.
Psalms—8:5; 68:17; 91:11; 103:20; 104:4; 148:2.
Isaiah—63:9.
Ezekiel—1:16, 19.
Daniel—3:28; 6:22.
Matthew—4:6, 11; 16:27; 18:10; 22:30; 24:31, 36; 25:31; 26:53.
Mark—1:13; 8:38; 12:25; 13:27, 32.
Luke—2:15; 4:10; 9:26; 12:8, 9; 15:10; 16:22; 20:36; 24:23.
John—1:51; 20:12.
Acts—7:53.
Romans—8:38.
I Corinthians—4:9; 11:10; 13:1.
Galatians—3:19.
Colossians—2:18.
II Thessalonians—1:7.
I Timothy—3:16; 5:21.
Hebrews—1:4-13; 2:2, 5, 7, 9, 16; 12:22; 13:2.
I Peter—1:12; 3:22.
II Peter—2:4, 11.
Revelation—1:20; 3:5; 5:11; 7:1-11; 8:2-13; 9:14, 15; 12:7-9; 14:10; 15:1-8; 16:1; 17:1; 21:9.

THE BOOKS OF ENOCH

"And Enoch walked with God."—*Genesis* 5:24

ONE of the most explicit descriptions of Angel Orders is found in the Apocryphal Books of Enoch.* Until recent centuries, portions of the writings of Enoch were included in the Old Testament. Monumental writings were excluded from the Bible during the Nicene Council assembly of the early Christian fathers (325 A.D.). Many of these works which were eliminated have since become known as "Books of the Apocrypha."

The etymology of the term "Apocryphal" springs from the root *crypto,* meaning "to hide." Thus some of the now excluded scriptures contain hidden or esoteric teachings which earlier Christian authorities believed were unsuited to popular understanding.

Enoch is believed to be a generic title designating a *seer.* In olden times, anyone possessing authentic seership was termed an "Enoch." Hence several seers are claimed to be the authors of the Books of Enoch.

At least three different versions of this esoteric scripture are known to Bible authorities. These differing translations have been found in the Hebrew, Ethiopian, and Grecian languages. The version considered most reliable is that of the Ethiopic manuscript.

The sincere seeker cannot read from these rare chapters without having his knowledge of Angelic Hosts vastly increased. They contain a gold mine of deeply inspired realities which make all who consider their meanings more enlightened seekers.

*3 *Enoch,* translated by Hugo Odeberg, Cambridge Univ. Press

Throughout the third volume of the Books of Enoch, in symbolical terms, the Angel Prince urges the prophet: "Come and I will show thee where the waters are suspended in the highest, where fire is burning in the midst of hail, where lightning lightens out of the midst of snowy mountains, where thunders are roaring in the celestial heights, where a flame is burning in the midst of a burning fire, and where voices make themselves heard in the midst of a thunder and the earthquake." (Chapter 42)

A student familiar with the language of symbolism will see in the foregoing passage a description of a dimension where polar opposites exist in united harmony. "Where the waters are suspended in the highest," symbolizes the highest plane of the astral world. *Water* is often used as a symbol of the fourth dimension. "Where fire is burning in the midst of hail, changes the locale to that of the *Causal* World. The Causal World is frequently likened to a dimension of fire, yet in the topography of that territory one observes crystal mountains from which fiery flashes issue and one hears sonorous chants of tremendous power. The Causal World contains treasuries of sound, energy, creative inspiration, and archetypal patterns of "things to come." Viewed from this aspect, this passage dealing with Causal observations becomes a lens through which we sight tidal events within this lofty level.

Our recorder informs us further regarding the gradations of celestial life: Angels, Archangels, Angel Princes, and Angel Kings. The latter are called "Rulers of the Eons." Those who have taken the Prince degree of

Angel initiation "have crowns of kinship to designate them from crowns of Glory."

Angel Princes of the highest rank are called *Watchers* and *Holy Ones,* or the "Irin and Qaddishin."

"Above all these are four great Princes, the Irin and Qaddishin by name; high, honored, revered, beloved, wonderful and glorious ones, greater than all the children of the heaven. There is none like unto them among all the servants, for each of them is equal to all the rest put together.

"And their dwelling is over against the Throne of Glory, and their standing place over against the Holy One, blessed be He, so that the brilliance of their dwelling is a reflection of the brilliance of the Throne of Glory. And the splendor of their countenance is a reflection of the splendor of Shekinah. (Shekinah means the Divine Manifestation of God's Presence or God's active Light.)

"And they are glorified by the glory of the Divine majesty and praised by the praise of the Shekinah." (Chapter 28)

According to the Third Book of Enoch, Metatron, the Angel Prince of the Presence, has access to the Divine Presence, the face of the Godhead, Who possesses knowledge of Divine Secrets and Decrees. He is a Prince of the Seventh Hall (plane), the inmost and holiest reach of the celestial world. He is an authority and judge of all the hosts of Angels and of those Angel Princes who are not above the entrance to the Seventh Hall. Metatron governs through His "sanctuary and altar"—an indication of extensive governing powers which originate from this Prince's own center, His Sanctuary.

69

The writings of Enoch reveal an order of Angelic Beings called the "Galgallim," known by the symbolical title, "The Wheel Beings." In the Old Testament, reference is made to the magnetic work which the Galgallim perform. "The appearance of the *wheels* and their work was like unto the color of beryl, and they four had one likeness; and their appearance and their work was, as it were, *a wheel in the middle of a wheel."—Ezekiel* 1:16

Evidently the Galgallim are of a very advanced order whose service is that of *creating centers of force* that resemble great wheels of moving energy. From Ezekiel's explanation, their activities extend throughout the inner planes.

Wherever there are important "chakras" in the body of this planet, Wheel Beings are present distributing specific powers. They would be found at the North and South Poles, as well as at certain points along the Equatorial line. The Galgallim even preside over Southern California at given places in order to help energize and sustain the new race work that is under development in this locality. Other beings of this order are in South America preparing it as the homeland of the coming Golden Age.

Another group of Angels introduced are the "Song-Uttering Angels": "At the time when the ministering Angels desire to say the song they first go down into the fiery stream and dip themselves in the cleansing fire. They dip their tongues and their mouths seven times. After that they go up and put on the garment of Light. They cover themselves with cloaks of Chasmal (Light substance) and stand in four rows over against the Throne of Glory in all the heavens." (Chapter 36)

70

"When the ministering Angels utter the Holy, then all the troops of consuming fire (Causal World inhabitants) and the fiery armies, and the flaming servants and the holy princes adorned with crowns, clad in kingly majesty, wrapped in glory, girt with loftiness, fall upon their faces three times, saying: 'Blessed be the name of His glorious kingdom forever!' " (Chapter 39)

When the Angels utter the Celestial Song of the Thrice Holy in the right order and manner, they are rewarded as it were, with crowns; and in the "fiery river" (of Light substance) the ministering Angels are renewed every morning.

"Whenever Angels utter a song at the wrong time, or as not appointed to be sung, they are burned and consumed by the fire (Light) of their Creator, and by a flame from their Maker and a whirlwind (a force) that blows upon them and throws them down into the fiery cleansing stream. But their spirit and their soul return to their Creator." (Chapter 47)

In addition to the Galgallim and the Song-Uttering Angels, Metatron explains that there are Angels of Justice, Mercy, Prayer, and Peace, as well as Archangels who are servants of His Throne and attendants of His Glory.

Frequent references are made to Shekinah—God's active Light. When Angels pray, they consciously enter the Shekinah, and because this is their practice, they have to realize a complete inner purification before praying. The mighty cleansing power of this eternal Light-in-action permeates even into the earth's zones when invoked: "For the splendor of the Shekinah traversed the world from one end to another with a radiance greater than that of the globe of the sun. And everyone who made use of the splendor of the Shekinah, on him no flies and no gnats did rest. Neither was he ill nor suffered he any pain. No demons got power over him, neither were they able to injure him." (Chapter 54)

We conclude our references to quotations about the Angels from the writings of Enoch with these magnificent words:

"There are numerous ministering Angels performing His Will (the Lord of the World), numerous Beings, Princes, in the Araboth of His delight—Angels who are revered among the rulers in heaven, distinguished, adorned with song and bringing love to remembrance, who are affrighted (awed) by the splendor of the Shekinah, and their eyes are dazzled by the shining beauty of their King." (Chapter 22)

"And even today, Angelic Orders are energetically carrying out the Will of the Highest, even now. They are gathering together and going down from heaven in parties, from the Throne in companies and from the heavens in camps to do His Will in the whole world." (Chapter 52)

The Books of Enoch contain not only a classical poetry of words, but a treasury of specific information, as we have seen. Rites of Song Angels are simply told so that even the newest student can follow the journey of these Angels into the astral planes where, level by level, they purify themselves. They finally reach the Causal plane where they consciously align themselves with their Bodies of Light (Soul forms) before uniting to utter together their holy chants.

The Shekinah described in Enoch's text refers to the

strong Light of the Causal level. Into this threshold only the pure and reverent may enter. All invocations for protection, healing and strengthening draw upon this mighty, intensely bright realm of creativity. Paul was transfixed by this Light which Jesus shone upon him from the Causal threshold.

We need often to reread Enoch's closing words, for they carry a potent attunement to the love and immediacy of God's Angelic Orders.

ACTIVITIES OF CELESTIAL INHABITANTS

ONE of the realizations which gives us a feeling of
expanded consciousness is the discovery that a line
of life evolves side by side with our human development
—a line whose bodies are composed of lighter substances
than our own, making them invisible to our heavier
sensibilities. Their influence and helpful ministrations
are most certainly shed upon man whether he is aware
of them or not. In the annals of sacred literature there
are many instances of Angelic Benefactors attending and
inspiring human beings.

By using a Bible Concordance, we can find under
the word, "Angel," innumerable references to descriptions in our own Christian Bible of the counsel, comfort,
protection and intervention the shining ones accorded
to patriarchs, disciples and apostles. In libraries we
should search for books along esoteric lines which contain indexes. Whenever we locate references to Angels,
we should read them and make notations of any new
or enlarged ideas that we receive from such research. It
would be an excellent practice to record in the unprinted
pages at the end of this volume our own experiences of
discovery either in reading or in our daily encounters
with them in meditation or moments of high inspiration.

Until the second century the early Christian fathers
taught that men are permeated by the influence and
kindness of Angelic Messengers. Leaders such as Chry-
sostom, Athanasius, Augustine, Irenaeus, Tertullian,

AN ALLSEE MOUNTAIN DEVA   DONALD E. BURSON

KING TREE DEVA   DONALD E. BURSON

A GUARDIAN ANGEL   JONATHAN WILTSHIRE

78

A WARRIOR ANGEL   JONATHAN WILTSHIRE

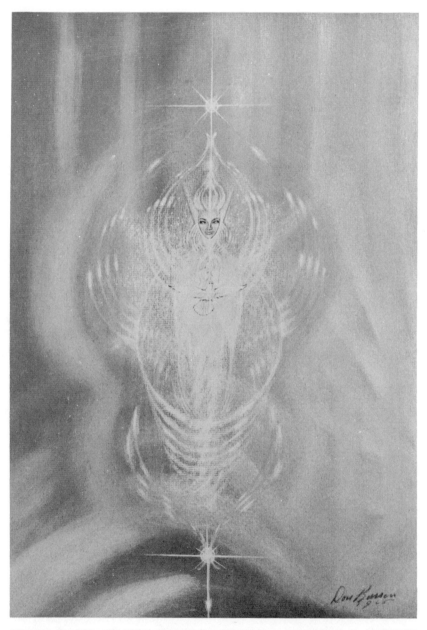

CHOHI ANGEL OF THE SPIRIT OF TRUTH   DONALD E. BURSON

AN ANGEL OF ENLIGHTENMENT   DONALD E. BURSON

AN AMENLEE ANGEL   JONATHAN WILTSHIRE

An Angel of the Morning

A Guardian Angel

An Angel of Prayer

An Angel of Music

An Angel of Birth

A Wind Angel

A Tree Deva

A Lord of Flame

A Race Spirit

91

Origen, Molina, Scotus, Bonaventura and Suarez accepted the fact of their guardianship. Ambrose stressed appreciation for the holy orders. At the fateful Council of Laodicea much that belonged to Christ's teachings was condemned, either as heresy or as doctrines unsuited for universal endorsement. The Phrygian group of Christians continued praising and blessing the ministry of Angels and their beliefs largely induced the church's return to a recognition of the Angelic Kingdom at the Lateran Council in 1215 A.D. Since this event in the thirteenth century, Christianity has embraced the missions of Angels and called them good.

St. Agatha received comfort from an Angelic Visitor during her prison confinement. When St. Christina was ill in a dungeon, an Angel of Healing ministered to her. St. Cecilia's music attracted the radiant ones and the musician was frequently aware of them as she played.

Handel is said to have experienced a rare religious exaltation during the composition of *The Messiah*. For twenty-four days he was completely withdrawn from the things of this world so that he "dwelt in the pastures of God." When the *Hallelujah Chorus* was completed a servant found him at the table with tears streaming down his cheeks. Afterward Handel explained, "I did think I did see all heaven open before me!"

Fra Angelico saw Angels in his meditations; and he discovered them in his room when he awoke from sleep. His paintings of these superphysical counselors were so inspired that no one has yet succeeded in achieving the unique spiritual quality he disclosed in his Angels. Angels were drawn without wings by earliest artists. Only the more recent paintings represented them with wings.

Michaelangelo and Raphael drew Angels without wings. It is well known to those with extended vision that the energy around the heavenly couriers moves so constantly and rapidly that, to the partially aware, this vibrant energy might easily be interpreted as wings. They certainly do not need feathered pinions—in the sense that birds need wings—to pilot them through space! The basis for much ridicule and unbelief stems from this common misconception.

St. Bartholomew voiced a truth when he mentioned that he noticed Angels exhaled fragrances. Angelic Beings can be distinguished by their fragrances. Healing Angels emanate that which resembles the scent of pine forests. Guardian Angels give us impressions of an inspiration lovelier than any of our flower perfumes. The fragrance of sandalwood denotes a presence who works along the lines full of creative instruction or healing.

William Blake beheld holy ones and put them into his poems and drawings. His pictures of Angels were so dramatic and accurate it appeared as if they had stood as models for Blake. This artist-poet one sunrise saw an innumerable host of Angels chanting, "Holy, holy, holy is Lord God Almighty!"

The more deeply we study the mysteries of Truth, the clearer and more natural to comprehension appears the Angelic path of life. At a certain point on each one's path of progress, life waves meet and blend. It is when this point is approached that students of spiritual realities begin to yearn for definite knowledge of these extended orders of God-Life. For is it not true that before a wise man travels widely he contemplates and mentally studies the places he hopes to visit? He may desire to see far-away places as intensely as a lover at sea craves to behold his beloved. Thus, too, when we are no longer satisfied with the limited confines of dogmatic or of purely mental conceptions, we will inwardly prepare ourselves to voyage into ever-widening oceans of awareness.

Angels execute their tasks with creative joy, unique resourcefulness, and colorful movement beyond anything comparable to human labors on earth. No drudgery infects their efforts. *They work with the joy of creating.* Fatigue and impatience never enter their states. Usually, after a duty is once assumed, it is acted upon tirelessly until its end is accomplished. The varying states such a task passes through is in itself most interesting. Once an Angel takes an endeavor into the domain of his attention, it will undergo numerous transitions, though the Angel involved may or may not have altered his position. I have observed a shining one who, for several days in a mountainous region, appeared in deep meditation which concerned protective work done on higher levels of consciousness for the mountain's safety from destructive elements.

Yet, I have also witnessed Nature Devas in groups of three, five or seven achieve similar protective measures by invoking powerful calls summoning Solar Light to encompass a specific locality with white flames of spiritual encirclement, for the purpose of repelling negative or destructive forces from entering such an area.

Angelic activities, in the main, are accompanied by flashing color "showers," rhythmical chants, and noticeably heightened frequencies. The tiniest elemental moving among the grasses in the fields or lowly wild flowers, sends out a miniature "lariat" which circles the grass blade or plant shoot he concentrates upon, filling it with two or three tones of pulsating color. Moreover, all the while this display of color-charging continues, a soft humming of the Song of Creation attends the workers.

Earth's electrical thunder storms are crashing dark monologues which compare poorly with the splendid outbursts of these "color storms" which gather, break and flash pointedly into special "fields" prepared especially by nature's supervising agents.

Illumined sages have long reverenced the mysteries connected with the sun. Their penetrating research separated "the chaff from the wheat" of mythology. From sage to successor through the ages we have learned that our physical sun is a tremendous vortex of force through which the invisible Solar Logos functions, sending His energies and directions among the planets of His solar system.

The highest initiates of every planet join with the loftiest ranks of certain Angelic Orders in entering consciously into sun service. Each dawn receptive earth persons can sense solar energies being released through the "screening" of myriad, myriad hosts of Sun Angels. Even our intuition reliably tells us that these mighty, pure ones who consecrate themselves to sun radiations are amazingly worthy and advanced intelligences.

Difficult as it is to try to describe these morning experiences, let me attempt a bird's-eye view of what is seen on an average morning. Paced with the pale dawn-radiance which begins to light the world around us each morning, is that inward acceleration which reaches us from Solar Angels. In color these radiations possess turquoise blue beams. Should they touch our auras, we would realize a blazing within ourselves of soulic force. Then, as the sun's rays rimmed the horizon, we should observe coral, orange and finally orange-yellow swells of color frequencies entering anew this region of our globe; and just before the sun "arose" in brilliant majesty, we should see hosts upon hosts of flaming figures, the nearest to our observation seeming to be the tallest and most radiant. Their voices would join in the Song of Creation with strong, victorious gladness. As the minutes passed, we should note the song becoming less intense. while for many measures their cadences would express the gentler gifts of renewed daily opportunities, endowments and ensoulments. Then a perceptible rising and strengthening of tones would again occur until a climax, rich in tones and blazing with Light, would enter the earth at the point of our perception.

Angels in Christ's endeavor strive explicitly to encourage and aid in man's spiritual re-creation. Their influence persists on the inward levels of being. By their ministrations our "wireless" apparatus of inner sensibilities is safeguarded, strengthened and supported until such time when outside aid is no longer necessary.

Many of the Angels who work for man's welfare use occasional ritualistic empowerment for their human "brothers." I have seen a Guardian Angel help her charge achieve a better degree of self-control under trying circumstances by calling into activity, through her Angelic thought, orange rings like whirling discs which moved up and down outside the orbit of the human's aura, creating not only an insulation to outside thoughts and influences, but likewise an incitement of the quality of courage.

At another time I watched a Guardian of a grief-stricken woman make in her own distinctive manner an invocation to her superiors for power with which to dispel the gloom of her charge. After three invocations to the Highest, each more glowing with Light emanations, the Guardian held up her right hand when she sensed power about to be released. With her left hand she sent flame-colored beams steadily into her charge's heart center. Within a few minutes the woman ceased crying and peace entered her eyes and body. As soon as relaxation in the woman was complete, the Guardian Angel changed her position. She put both of her hands on the head of the depressed woman (her right hand lightly on top of her left hand) and contemplated a life program the widow could best follow. When the model of this design was finished it scintillated vital blue energy. Then into the mental body, particularly into the region of the sixth and seventh chakras (centers) the Angel projected this pattern. As the woman began to receive the accelerations of this archetype her aura brightened, while she began considering the ways and means she would develop to carry out these (implanted) ideas.

The *Layman's Magazine* tells of the remarkable rescue of Donn Fendler of Rye, New York, apparently a Guardian Angel's answer to prayer. The boy, twelve years of age, wandered from a party on Mt. Katahdin in Maine one summer and for nine days was lost in the trackless wilderness. He was without compass, matches or knife, tormented and stung by mosquitoes, without food of any kind except berries, and in danger of wild animals. Finally he fell on his face exhausted, starving, half blind, with one foot injured. "At this moment, when he no longer had strength to raise himself out of the mud, he prayed and his prayer was answered. He felt hands on his shoulders lifting him. He cried out with joy, thinking that some guide had found him. But no one was in sight. Yet the pressure of hands continued, lifting, lifting, until he stood upon his own feet, and covered the last few miles to safety."

I recall observing a Prayer Angel's efforts regarding a human being's prayers for the welfare of loved ones during a long absence. As the pink winged thought-form moved from the pray-er in the direction of his home, a stately Prayer Angel arrested the home-going thought. After several moments it appeared as though a searchlight of purest white Light shone directly above the mental image. Slowly the image began to expand, to increase its size, and change in color from a glowing pink to a white-pink, "breathing" form. Tracing this prayer form to its destination, I saw it tended and guarded by the beloved Angel of the Place. She added Her own flame encirclement about the human prayer which emitted an exquisite fragrance as well as pulsating vitality.

In *The Kingdom Digest* is found a case of Divine intervention concerning a Roumanian. Count Michael lay wounded on the battlefield. All around him were Germans. With the return of consciousness the soldier began to wonder how he could reach his own lines. If he were observed moving in the direction of his own forces, he would be taken prisoner or shot. Phrases from the ninety-first Psalm stirred in his memory—"He is my refuge . . . He shall deliver me . . . *He shall give His*

Angels charge over me . . . He will make me to abide under the shadow of the Almighty." As these verses lighted his consciousness, the Roumanian had a strong urge to make a break for his lines. He moved forward as if guided, for a heavy mist seemed to envelop him and obscure his vision. Everywhere Germans encircled him, yet he made the return to his own trenches, much to the astonishment of his men. The Roumanian sentries who were watching the battlefield observed this soldier advancing toward them in a uniform unlike that of the enemy, and were at a loss to understand their comrade's miraculous protection. To all appearances, their compatriot had been made invisible to the enemy! God's means for helping man are strange, but always effectual. No doubt the soldier's prayer invoked the help of an Angel to aid him in his extreme emergency.

Initiations enter into Angelic evolution just as they do into human unfoldment. Elementals receive minor and major ordinations of Soulic power as they journey upward stage by stage to attain at last the title of Angel. Then begin numerous initiations of ever-increasing intensities which take an Angel upward through many assigned tasks and inward illuminations until all the steps of an Angel's special path have been experienced. His initiations proceed into those of Archangel, Angel Prince, and Angel King (called Eon) degrees. Altogether, initiation begins sooner within the Angel Kingdom than in the human way; it contains many more thresholds to conquer and the conferring of many more degrees than human's meet.

As peculiar to his entire earth incarnation, man meets purifications through suffering even within the sacred moments of soul initiation (enlightenment of consciousness). With humans initiation brings the necessity of renunciations and the gaining of new levels of consciousness. With Angelic evolution, initiatory degrees enlarge individual consciousness and inaugurate and strengthen new abilities needful to the missions and fields of service allotted one. In man, initiation means deepened insight and added self-conquest. To an Angel, initiation brings joyous progress on to higher duties and more expanded service. An Angel grows by including more territory within the sphere of his helpfulness.

Angels possess natural preferences which permit them to develop along lines most suited to their temperaments. Those who need the "climate" of high voltage currents become Power Angels. Guardian Angels prefer specialization and growth through detailed and patient watchfulness. Great Nature Devas whose site of endeavor may be a mountain peak in a quiet, remote region, require isolation from human crowds and cities because their work is wholly related to supervising, ensouling and guarding the elemental lives devoted to the inner care of nature's forces.

Angels have their peers and Spiritual Hierophants and Regents in a manner comparable to those of human beings. An Angel's response to a reception of empowerment or direction from his Lord causes his aura and centers of consciousness to glisten with fiery or gleaming colors. Angels are instantly responsive to suggestions from their advisors. They are also aware of the specific sender of an order or a baptism of power which they receive. Deva temples are centers where strong wonderful surges of multicolors and of fragrant incense are broadcast by individual Angels or groups up to Those Who Are Yet Higher.

In our own ways let us find time for expressing devotion and appreciation to that other line—the Angel path of evolution whose services are so inexorably woven into the very core of human existence. They do not seek or wish *worship*, knowing that alone belongs to the Infinite Creator-Creatrix of life. They do welcome our remembrance of their respective interests—nature, the creatures, and evolving man. Our wiser care of those things which embody their interests shall strengthen our intuitional awareness of their activities. Our inward and outward strivings receive new encouragement every time we pause to deeply consider Angelic magnitudes of selfless service performed in "the beauty of holiness."

When humans face testings and tragedy, they should remember the Angels who are always standing ready to lend their celestial assistance, comfort and counsel.

MAN'S RELATION TO ANGELIC ORDERS*

WITH many weighty world problems absorbing the attention of humanity, it might seem odd to mention the reality of Angels—especially in a century so given to intellectual and scientific pursuits. Yet, that which is true belongs to every age, and every race has need of its helpfulness. While scientists study atomic energy and astronomers search for faraway planets, men are unmindful of powers which are far greater and nearer than those which can be reached by atom-smashers or giant telescopes. If men would learn more about the use of the sixth sense within them, they could embark upon such adventures as are now inconceivable.

The mystics, sages and prophets of all the ages were telepathically aware of sciences and realities which might astound the materially intellectual mind. They witnessed the presences, instructions and blessings of the Angels.

In appearance, the celestial inhabitants are quite different from ourselves. In every respect they are larger than humans. One must adjust himself to new conceptions of size in order to appreciate the higher ones. There are Angels thirty feet in height and we have seen great Nature Lords whose bodies were as huge as the mountains they enshrouded. This is true of the Being who envelops Mt. Rainier. The faces of most of the Angelic Beings are rather pointed. Their eyes can be likened to flashes of lightning. Angels imbibe electricity from the etheric regions and this sustains them in the same way we inbreathe oxygen. The impression one has

*Excerpts from *Eternal Verities,* now out of print.

while observing these pure beings is a yearning for the tremendous vitality with which they are endowed. The celestial workers are always joyous, confident and sympathetic. This is natural when we realize their ever-present attunement to the Power of the Most High.

The ministering ones who surround us minutely are almost too numerous for description. We are in the presence of City, State and National Angels. We are always encouraged when we notice the recognition of these Angels as we enter various cities and states on our frequent lecture tours. Of the Weather Angels who affect us, there are Angels of Calm, Storm and Wind. The Electric Angels are more difficult to perceive but we are aware of their force affecting our planet. In the outdoors we have observed Angels of the mountains, valleys, oceans, lakes and waterfalls. Whenever we go into the hills or forests we are filled with the spirit of expectant perception. We are never disappointed, for always are the Angels just as eager to be realized as we are desirous of their contact.

Despite the tumultuous, mercenary qualities which emanate from a great metropolis, far above its heavy aura a strong Angel resides. The spiritual, cultural and artistic activities in a city respond to the quickening of such a presence. Through whatever pure channels the Angel of a City can radiate its Light, the populace is reached, however unknowingly. No place is too material or too evil to repel the appointed servitors of the Divine Will. Often on Sundays I have observed great Christ Angels blessing the cities they overshadow. On the Sabbath Day, material thought waves subside while spiritual frequencies are gathered and distributed by great presences who are responsible for the city's spiritual charging.

The Healing Angels respond to prayers for healing. A definite appeal for aid brings them to the side of the sick. I have watched these workers, whose auras are medium blue, while they combed the auras of the sick for whom they were summoned. When the astral and physical bodies are stirred by cleansing, the life force enters harmoniously and the ill become well again. Healing Angels also work with those who do not seek spiritual healing. They inspire doctors and direct nurses as to how to care for those in their charge, telepathically advising the right administrations for each case. However, when the particular cycle under which the human labors reaches its culmination, whether that be in childhood or maturity, the Healing Angels do not interfere with the law governing transition.

The Angels of Prayer have white auras. They attend to the thought forms created by meditations or prayers. They guard a constructive thought so that it will progress free from interference. Unworthy appeals never reach their levels. Our prayers are like seeds which have their seasons of blossoming and of fruitfulness. The love which guards and nourishes our inspirations is something for which we can always be grateful.

At every spiritual service, we are attended by the beautiful Religious Angels. They are the most joyous beings I have ever observed. Entire audiences are gathered into the auras of these workers. Soon the audience is suffused by an atmosphere of changing colors. Each speaker is particularly helped by the power directed to him from these invisible helpers.

All persons are watched by some type of ministering soul. Children are in the custody of Watcher Angels. The most loving instructor we can contact intimately is the Guardian Angel. Guardians are our Celestial Mothers. Not until we decide to live earnestly and nobly do we attract the attention of one who becomes our Guardian. This shining being usually remains with us constantly from our entrance upon the path until we successfully pass our fifth initiation. Guardians have pink or rose colored auras, the lighter color denoting Divine affection.

In many tests, I have noticed that Guardians become the initiators. When a disciple passes the third initiation, the Guardian is silent and the Master becomes the initiator. The Guardian Angel communes with the Higher Self and teaches it to become more actively conscious. Some Guardians announce themselves by fragrances, others by certain colorful symbols. One friend realizes her Guardian's presence because of the perfume of lilies-of-the-valley suddenly becoming noticeable in the air around her.

When I have been confused and apparently lost in the mountains, I have always received accurate instructions from this loyal instructress. My love and respect for my Guardian Angel is second only to the depth of feeling I know for God and the Lord Jesus.

Frequently after a lecture some awakened person explains, "Intuitively I felt urged to attend this service. Now I realize what I was sent to receive." Usually high above the student's head is a face, radiant with tender understanding. This is the devotee's Guardian Angel. Many times such an Angelic Being nods to me after an

106

individual's explanation as though to designate, "I am the one responsible for this soul's intuition."

The world has yet to attune itself to the higher sound waves which carry the symphonies and choirs of the celestial realm. It is helpful to practice listening when at the seashore, or while meditating near a musical brook. Sometimes a reflection of their harmonies can even be heard in the overtones of the water.

How interesting it is to find Angels cheering, uplifting and purifying worlds of song! The Angels of Song always direct their anthems toward planets on which there are human beings. I have noticed that on Sundays and Sacred Holidays their harmonies are heard more distinctly than on other days when men's materialistic thoughts create interference, similar to static which hinders radio reception.

The Celestial Choruses work together in great numbers. Their singing can be likened to humming for they express tones, without words. Wagner received much of his inspiration from his sensitive reception of these heavenly concerts. In visiting the bedsides of those who were gravely ill, I have often noticed certain chants being directed toward these persons. Women who are giving birth to an advanced soul are often uplifted on waves of triumphant song. Though but a child during World War I, I distinctly remember that wounded soldiers always carried with them a strain of music resembling a march. This melody would repeat itself over and over again until, at the soldier's recovery of health, the music would become so faint it would go beyond my hearing.

In several department stores and factories, I have found that people work to a definite rhythm. Now I know that all forms of constructive activities are sent the harmonizing and encouraging influence of music. I recall a magazine article describing the following incident: Three persons met one morning before an orthodox church. One of the persons was an organist, on an errand to the church. As this person and his friends talked, they were startled by sounds of music coming from the auditorium of their church. The three persons listened attentively, wondering who could be using the organ. As impressions were compared, it was agreed that the music sounded more like singers humming than organ notes. The organist unlocked the church and the three stared into the chapel. No one was there! The surprised organist and his friends perhaps never learned the source of this mysterious music. They did not realize that every temple or center wherein the Divine Presence is recognized and worshipped is always purified and recharged by Angelic Presences.

These observations and experiences may awaken the reader's desire for contact with the Angelic Ones. As we develop through noble and unselfish efforts, we shall draw nearer to them, and at the same time they will be patiently awaiting and seeking our recognition. To those who do not have this direct contact as yet, I would suggest these steps:

1. Study literature which contains mention of the Angels. Familiarize yourself with all the known realizations about them.
2. Keep a prayer in your heart that you will be drawn into an association with one who sees and understands the great ones. Strive to so live that your teachers will seek to become your friends.

3. Once each year take a pilgrimage into nature and there practice sending the Angels love, devotion, and your receptivity.

4. Every day be eager to feel the guidance and the nearness of the shining ones. Be grateful for the slightest token of their helpfulness.

Several times I have been asked, "What do you consider is the greatest benefit in seeing an Angel?" Happily I have answered, "To see but one glorified being is to always remember the meaning of beauty, the power of love, and the blessedness of sincerity. The sight of one who reflects the Light more completely and consciously than ourselves, is our challenge to greater effort."

We are usually eager to expand the circumference of our friendships on the outer plane. Why should we limit our companionships? We should be enthusiastic to widen the scope of our contacts until, through ceaseless searching, our love includes the limitless hosts of all the workers in the service of God.

Natives of Eternity

THE KINGDOM OF ANGELS

STRANGE wonders permeate our world, sublime mysteries almost too pure for our full understanding. Our planet, and its atmosphere, is not only pervaded by invisible radio-active waves and silent, potent rays, but by shining beings whose ceaseless ministries enliven and uplift us. More wonderful than the far-reaching effects of television, or the harnessing of the inimitable cosmic rays, will be our recognition of these glorious presences. Since time unfurled its amazing creation, Angelic Beings have nurtured the advancement and unfoldment of man. References to them have usually been accepted with amusement and disbelief. Behind every ageless belief, however, lies a hidden reality whose meaning should be sought with earnestness. Our ignorance of Angels does not make them non-existent, it only closes us to their existence. Our yearning to realize them opens us to their association.

The Angelic Kingdom, like the human kingdom, is a path of evolving life. It is composed of beings whose bodies, compared to ours, are etheric. The purpose underyling Angelic unfoldment is perfection through joyousness and service. The human way is impelled toward the development of love and wisdom. Those who inhabit the celestial kingdom are free from strife and evil. Human beings are strengthened by their overcoming the forces of discord and malice within themselves. Angels are immortal; human beings require the rest of death to prepare them for new cycles of self-expression. The way of Angelic evolution is exacting and long, whereas that of human wayfarers, though strenuous, is comparatively short. The more man associates with nature, the purer his vibrations, because nature beings have no destructive emotions. All is done consciously from the highest and purest levels.

There are numerous celestial orders, many of which we know very little about. The groups from whom we receive ministrations are:

1. The Angels of Nature
2. The Builders of Form
3. The Angels of Inspiration
4. The Angels of Love
    a. Guardian Angels
    b. Healing Angels
    c. Religious Angels
    d. Song Angels
5. The Angels of Birth and Death

The Angels devoted to nature cause a continuous renaissance in that kingdom. They supervise the elements and the seasons of our year. The law of cause and effect ordains the kind of ministry the earth deserves to receive. They cannot prevent earthquakes or floods, but they can bring rain or calm to a worthy region. Our careless neglect of soil conservation throughout the central states brought about many weeks of devastating dust storms. When mankind ignorantly or heedlessly commits an error, the Angels of Nature are not permitted to interfere with the accompanying compensation men attract in soil erosion. Were the great ones allowed to prevent such catastrophies, we would not learn our lesson concerning the right use and care of the blessings with which nature is endowed.

THE KINGDOM OF ANGELS

The Builders of Form, unlike the Angels of Nature, are not in our atmosphere. The thoughts of these architects direct the planning and construction of manifestations that appear as new types of minerals, vegetables, animals, or men. They work entirely from the fifth dimension which is a realm devoted wholly to mental quests.

A colorful group of figures are the glowing Angels of Inspiration. Their auras are the shade of flaming sunsets, which contrast greatly with the contemplative serenity of their faces. Their intense feeling for beauty is expelled in vibrant thought forms they send earthward. These celestial impressions later appear in such melodic prayers as the opening strains of Wagner's *Lohengrin*. Inspired thoughts are entwined with the imagery of artists and poets that the ideal might be revealed as a beatitude. These divine dreamers may draw the spirit of a composer to their fervent levels or they might visit the sanctum of creative effort. The Angels of Inspiration seldom reveal themselves since they concentrate one-pointedly on the flow of lyrical ideas or harmonies reaching an aspiring individual.

The mystic announcement of sunrise sends forth a blessing before which all forms pertaining to the nature kingdom stand expectant and reverent. Resplendent colors mingled with the sound effects of the esoteric dawn herald the good tidings of a new day. Through the beauty of sunrise vibrate the incantations of the Angels of the Morning. They are emissaries from the Solar Logos whose task is to direct the spiritual radiations of the sun to this planet revolving before them.

The celestial workers who serve us directly and who

keep nearer to us than most of the Angelic Orders are the Angels of Love. They are dedicated to the ministry of our guidance, healing, upliftment and harmony. Guardian Angels are beings who devote their time and efforts to our inner unfoldment. We do not attract the attention of these selfless ones until we are consciously seeking God's vast plan and purpose regarding us. When our yearning for self-conquest and wisdom grows intense, a Guardian Angel takes her place at our right side. Through her direction, understanding and overshadowing we are led to the various leaders and teachers we require for our inner training.

A Guardian is of great importance to our higher progress. The Guardian Angel stands next to the Master who is the teacher of our ray or path. Her advice speaks in our intuitions and her teachings in our deepening convictions. She leads us into the long corridor of overcoming, and when once within that hall of testing, she becomes our examiner and our initiator. As time advances us, the Guardian refrains more and more from counseling us. She remains with us during the lengthy process of our inner instruction, but at the first indication of our readiness to think and act independently, she withdraws her influence. Thereafter she remains with us as a protectress—a compass directing our footsteps. At any time our consciousness is clouded, hers is the clarifying current sweeping the mind of negative debris.

Guardian Angels are truly like patient, older sisters who uphold and direct us, and administer correction or encouragement whenever necessary. The strange ways in which they aid worthy charges is recorded in several instances in the Bible. In *Matthew* 1:20 an Angel ap-

116

pears to Joseph. Likewise, in *Matthew* 2:13 an Angel warns Joseph to flee into Egypt. In the *Acts* 5:19 Guardians open a prison door; and in 12:7 an Angel releases Peter from prison. In 27:22 of the *Acts* an Angel warns Paul of shipwreck. The Bible makes numerous references to these loving servers whose faces are clothed with the radiance of those who know God. Guardians can be distinguished from other Angelic Orders by the golden radiation about the heart center, and by the pale pink auras which encircle them.

An interesting service is rendered by the Healing Angels. Theirs is the task of clearing the congested areas in our etheric bodies so that the flow of cosmic energies can affect the inner as well as the outer man. These workers are clothed in light blue radiations, and the color of the emanations from them signifies their service.

Hospitals and sanitariums are enfolded in the healing Light which these Angels create. The thought atmosphere about a place of suffering would be so heavy and dark that the finer powers could scarcely enter, were it not for the Healing Angels who, by their strong, pure, tranquilizing influence, equalize or change the surrounding atmosphere. They work for depression to be replaced by hope, and for pain to give way to peace.

There are at least three Healing Angels always about a hospital, but the prayers of individual patients or the devotions of anxious relatives often invite beings who accept single cases. They first ascertain whether a patient is to be released from the body, or healed. If their investigation reveals that the person's life span is not finished, they first arrest the illness and then work to enlighten the consciousness of the patient. They inspire

117

doctors with the proper diagnosis and the right treatment. Whether a medical man prescribes or a metaphysician prays, help from the higher dimensions attends the afflicted. The coming new race, through telepathy, will be able to tune into the powers from the Healing Angels as assuredly as we now attune ourselves to our favorite radio program. Then the Angels will inform us of the obscure causes of our weaknesses, and with them teaching us how to heal the effects, we shall attain an unwavering healing consciousness.

The presences that enfold audiences wherever the Spirit of God is worshiped are called Religious Angels. These servants of devotion appear in a cathedral, chapel, hall or home when invocation is made to the Power of the Most High. When a chapel is empty, at least two workers remain to increase the silent influences of the church. During a service, however, each group attracts from three to twelve Angels whose delightful duty it is to utilize the devotional outpouring of the gathering. They direct these energies from the temple to the entire community so that passers-by not interested in religion will nevertheless receive an inner peace as they travel through these charged emanations.

During a service the Religious Angels strive to awaken passive persons into an active use of spiritual principles. The discouraged are relieved of their self-concern. Those searching for the Truth are given special guidance through a statement the minister or leader is impelled to utter. Were worshipers aware of the luminous figures above them, they would witness beauty impossible to describe. They would notice great faces peering down at them from billows of opal and coral diffusions. Time will open the heavy eyelids of our spirits that we may witness God's glory about us.

Occasionally we have heard about the "music of the spheres" without comprehending the full meaning of the term. In the Kingdom of the Angels exists an order consecrated to music. This order is not composed of an orchestra, but a choir. The songs are given out as chants; many of them are heard in march time. The magnitude of this choir is almost inconceivable; still more difficult to realize are the various octaves and keys in which this great assembly sings. Angels do not use vocal cords for speech or song. They speak from the mind and sing from the heart. When heard, their melodic variations are almost overpowering. The enthralling effects hymns of praise, courage, gratitude, love and worship have upon our world are very great. The ears of our inner man are always attuned to the Music of the Spheres. Our inmost selves are ever aware of the rhythmic cadences filling the higher dimensions, as natural to those realms as bird notes are to ours. All the experiences of man, Angel and God are expressed in these unending chants. Human composers have heard their songs depicting growth through struggle, the joyousness of love, and the benediction of self-mastery. Their chants are directed to those laboring in factories, to those chafing in prison, to those who brave the anguish of pain. The sunrise hour of Easter attunes throngs to their triumphant praises. Alone, an individual aspirant in moments of stress, heroism or illumination is inwardly aligned with the chorus singing the anthem he requires for courage, balance or serenity. Though the reception of the heavenly music is seldom relayed to the conscious mind, the effects of the songs upon the inner self are noticeable by a surging and enlivening of the higher states of consciousness.

Were we capable of perceiving the Angels of Song, we would witness hosts of glorious singers whose auric emanations form a diverging rainbow of soft or bright hues, according to the tones of their songs. Wagner must have been very sensitive to the intonations of Angelic singers, for his scores reflect their songs quite clearly. Cesar Franck, a mystic of the arts, surely heard celestial overtones, for his music carries their transcendent message.

A glimpse of many Music Devas occurred while attending a symphony in one of Southern California's loveliest and largest outdoor amphitheaters. During the first selections of the evening a great number of Music Angels were visible guiding the inner forces of melodic sounds into great streams of power which encircled the group. As the opening bars of Stravinsky's *The Firebird* were announced, a Great Figure enshrouded the multitudinous audience. In this one's radiations, everything seemed more alive, stronger and more enchanting. Never had music revealed its true meaning to me as clearly as it did while I listened enthralled that night. This glorious visitor affected others in the assembly too, as the enrapt people appeared singularly attentive. At the conclusion of the number the figure vanished. "Evidently," I remarked to my sympathetic companion, "that being was intent upon helping to usher in new forms of music. The visitor must have been a masterly influence whose task is to bring us those harmonies that stir the intuitional qualities in man. The novel number,

The Firebird, contains the staccato notes that resound like knocking upon the gates of inner mysteries."

On our human pilgrimage, we are confronted by the supreme moments of birth and death. These passages are directed by beings of an eminent administrative degree. In size, beauty and development they are superior to the Angels already mentioned. The inhabitants of all the celestial dimensions are sustained by a peculiar inbreathing of that energy we call electricity. The Angels of Birth and Transition, like other Angels, understand how to inhale vivifying properties, but they possess an added capacity. They use electrical force to unite a soul with his infant body at birth, and to free him from his physical body at death. Only at these momentous junctures do we *see* the illustrious figures renowned for their wisdom, compassion and power. The last impression we have before we are plunged into the dimension of matter is that of a beatific face encircled by an aureole of blinding Light. The first presence to greet us as we cross the threshold of transition is that of the hallowed releaser. The wonders of birth and death are eclipsed by the momentary glimpses of the supernal pilots.

Beings from the celestial kingdom enter our kingdom, in human bodies, for various reasons. They are usually attracted by a curiosity to learn about those influences that enlighten us. Frequently those who enter our world are bewildered by our customs and routines. Consequently these visitors seem ill-fitted in our material world.

One of the most beautiful women of my acquaintance unveiled her origin to me by her illuminating comments.

She remarked, "Though I have every reason to be happy with a devoted husband, lovely children, a beautiful home, and worthwhile friends, I feel imprisoned by my environment. In nature, I am like a bird freed from a cage. Throughout my associations with others and my reactions to material problems, I seem to see things as though I viewed them from the 'outside.' My husband and associates view situations as if they were looking at them from an 'inside' perspective. Am I unnatural? Should I learn to orient myself to their viewpoint?"

While the speaker had been analyzing herself, a flash of intuition enlightened me as to her identity. She was a Nature Angel, dissatisfied in this world. Slowly and carefully I explained my realizations to the anxious woman. Her eyes filled with the light of understanding as she said, "You have revealed the wellspring of my being. Knowing that I am a visitor here on a sacred quest will give me patience, tolerance and appreciation for the world I am visiting."

I am of the opinion that Marie Corelli, Olive Schreiner, and Vaslaw Nijinsky were beings from the nature line of evolution. A significant incident disclosed to me the homeland of the world's greatest dancer. On page 342 of the book *Nijinsky*, by Romola Nijinsky, is the account of a foot injury Nijinsky received. An X-ray unveiled the fact that Vaslaw's feet were not formed like that of other human beings anatomically; in fact they were a combination of man and bird construction. The doctor exclaimed, "This is the secret of his amazing elevation; no wonder he can fly; he is a human bird."

Occasionally beings from the celestial realms enter our dimension to perform some special service. This I believe, was true of Joan of Arc. There are times when the radiant ones find it necessary to give us help in concrete ways. Twice, while traveling, I had occasion to rejoice in their saving us from possible death. One foggy night, during my early childhood, my mother and I drove with a married couple through the Pocono Mountains of Pennsylvania. A flashing signal from my Guardian was a warning to the driver urging him to immediately stop the car. No sooner had he done so than a night flyer whizzed past us. Sleepiness as well as the heavy fog prevented us from seeing the railroad crossing which was not clearly indicated. The four of us have never forgotten that night of grave danger and miraculous escape.

Years ago when on a lecture tour my husband and I faced sudden death on a busy highway. In the crucial moment we were conscious of a power that literally shoved our car into a soft snowbank. An exclaiming group of persons gathered, marveling at our deliverance. They found us deeply touched by this verification of invisible intervention.

Two very dear friends shared an extraordinary happening with us, trusting that we would understand its meaning more readily than they did. This middle-aged couple drove late one night through a desolate swamp region of Georgia. At this inopportune hour they had a punctured tire. Mr. G. searched uncertainly through his new car for tools. Unfortunately he carried no flashlight, which added to the strain of searching on a very dark night. It was finally decided that they would need help from some passing motorist who possessed a pocket light. The highway was devoid of cars when Mrs. G. suggested that they pray for help and protection. Although they had not seen a single car for more than an hour, they had scarcely opened their eyes when a touring car approached them. The driver of the car stopped and of his own will sprang lightly to the side of our grateful friends. The person who had volunteered his assistance was a young man who appeared tall, lean, and abounding in vitality and good humor. His significant greeting, "It is not safe for you to have trouble in this desolate place," later gave the couple reason for reflection. Without further remarks, the young helper busied himself about the car while Mr. G. held the searchlight brought over from the other car. Within a few minutes the youth said, "The car is now ready; you may be on your way."

Mr. G. extended a generous bill to the kindly youth. It was declined with the remark, *"I have no need for that."* When our friends were comfortably seated in their car, they were going to call out a friendly farewell to their rescuer when they suddenly realized there was no car and no person anywhere in sight. Two wide-eyed persons peered up and down the highway. "Why, that is odd," said Mr. G. "It is almost unaccountable! What do you suppose became of our knight errant? Perhaps he represented some special providence . . . I wish we knew." In hearing of this incident I recognized at once that the prayers of these two unselfish persons had attracted the attention of a willing server.

Intimate knowledge of the inhabitants of the Angelic Kingdom follows our longing for confirmation. The very fact that their existence is brought to our attention, indicates a readiness on our part to enter the threshold of discovery. Before we can attain sight of crystalline

124

levels, our consciousness must be purified, layer by layer. Sincerity, aspiration, and singleness of purpose, rather than chastity, dispel the fog of negative attitudes. The effort necessary to inner sight is not a matter of strength or determination, but rather of character development and a positive receptivity. These qualifications unfold through meditation and an exercise of the inner faculties in man.

To the aspirant, daily meditation is as essential as nourishing food. Regularity in this practice brings us a sense of an ever-widening consciousness. Meditation is the laboratory in which our Higher Selves are alchemists. One by one the baser elements in our interests and desires are transmuted, until the tone and movement of our energies follow an upward trend. By contemplating the joyousness and selflessness they know, our natures begin to reflect some of their Light, thus bringing us into rhythm with them. Each period of purposeful thoughtfulness deepens and enkindles our inner sensibilities.

The phases which receive our attention during meditation follow these general lines:

1. Devotion to the practice of self-mastery.
2. Perseverance in remembering the goal of our aspiration.
3. The practice of awareness.

The uncontrolled and uncultivated regions of our natures require daily consideration. Anger, intolerance and hatred weight us heavily with a gravitating influence. We must plan and carry out an elimination of destructive forces. Self-satisfaction, doubts and ignorance must be uprooted under our patient scrutiny. Measures should be taken for the mapping of our hourly overcomings. The price we pay in fruitful self-conquest is reasonable in comparison to the inestimable values we receive on our ascendant journey.

Should the discipline of our wayward thoughts and fancies seem arduous, our efforts can be reinforced. Reflection upon the luminous reality of Angels spurs us on to attainment. As freqently as possible we should take walks along unfrequented paths. Our being alone is essential. Before we embark upon an inviting trail, we should reflect, "This walk is dedicated to the recognition of God in everything about me. I will look upon all scenes with the realization, 'God breathes through these trees, from that mountain, and in the fields. His is the spirit that moves the birds to sing and the wind to croon.' I will be so occupied with watching and listening that should some presence enfold me, I will feel and see it, too." Then, as we leisurely walk, we are so filled by an attentiveness to the Highest that our own Infinite Selves look through the open door of our observation upon the world. Our minds are clarified, our emotions synchronized to the heartbeat of exultation, and slowly our physical sight is intensified by spiritual sight, and the countryside before us appears to be a gleaming spectacle of unimaginable beauty and life. There silhouetted against the brightness of this pictorial revelation are great, colorful beings whose slightest administrations express a vibrant, effervescent quality unknown to man.

With each advent into nature an enlarging conception and appreciation of eternal realities reawakens in us. The habit of awareness must be cultivated so that in any suitable place, in the home, in a garden, or in a temple, our consciousness can enter the higher kingdom enveloping us. When entrance to the vaster dimensions is made, our endeavor then consists of maintaining that awareness in all the departments of our lives.

What an infinitesimal fraction of the glories enveloping us do we ordinarily perceive! Sustained aspiration and constructive training will widen the circumference of our sight. Our realizations will include the limitless orders unfolding within the Pristine Spirit. How beautiful it will be to sense God in all His manifestations! Wonderful, too, will be our joining the procession made of united men and Angels whose reverent praises to the Highest reverberate throughout the universe.

THE ANGELS OF NATURE

M AN is a recipient of gracious gifts that come to him hourly through the glories and favors of nature. He is indirectly influenced and enriched by the ministry of those shining presences that are called the Angels of Nature.

Everywhere we witness the work of this important group of Angels, for they keep the earth green, productive and beautiful. The wind, weather and landscape conform to their movements and directions. Even the transition of the seasons is influenced by certain orders who have charge of the quarterly changes.

Fluctuating about us momently are the Angels of the Elements. This group has many divisions, for all Angelic life evolving through the earth, fire, air and water kingdoms at some period serves nature. The Weather Angels are either Devas of Wind, Storm or Calm. The Angels of the Seasons each have their own way of vivifying or making dormant the life they protect. The Angels of Harvest hover over areas raising food necessary to the human race. One of our first realizations concerning nature is that certain localities are used as charging centers. Thus a virgin forest, a mountain peak, or a quiet lake might be the reservoir of great spiritual energy. One forest will be vibrant with healing energies which are especially invigorating to the etheric body. Another mountain fastness will possess a strong current of reverence for God. Lake regions are usually attuned to radiations of peace. The open desert country quickens keenness of mind. These contrasting vibrations are

129

largely due to the types of beings which ensoul the various territories.

Occasionally when hiking in canyons or mountainous regions I have been attuned to the exuberant calls the Mountain Devas shout to each other across chasms or ridges. Every mountain chain has its directing Lord, as well as its numerous Angelic Guardians which are often called "The Spirits of the Mountains." These beings work toward stirring the languor of plant life into the activity of growth. In truth they are the impetus that quickens the lungs of nature. The sizes of these Guardians of the Summits vary from an average height of ten feet to that of a hundred feet or more. Nature Lords are as large as the mountains they enshroud.

When one with extended faculties enters the boundaries of Mt. Rainier National Park, the peals of resonant bells are heard which gradually diminish as one travels deeper into this renowned park. Imperceptible at first, and then with increasing clarity, radiations of deepest reverence are distinguished. Gradually the woodland spirits are seen, all traveling in one general direction. An atmosphere of complete devotion and veneration permeates the on-going procession. Upon the higher elevations, three tiers of beings can be observed slowly moving upward, singing their hymns of praise in a great crescendo of celestial harmony.

At a point near the mountain peak, the nature spirits gather to stand in hushed awe before the altar of their Lord. As certain hosts conclude their adorations, they are replaced by those who stand behind them. Thus the processional of worship continues unbroken upon that majestic mountainside.

THE ANGELS OF NATURE

Overshadowing the snow-capped dome is the actual head and face of the Lord of Mt. Rainier. He turns slowly so that He may evenly bless all the areas over which He has charge. When the morning dawns, His face is toward the sunrise. By the afternoon He is facing the Paradise Valley area. There are no descriptions in the human language which can justly picture Him. But to one with extended vision His expression of serenity and compassion is unforgettable. The Lord of the Mountain is as understanding of human beings as He is of the Devas in His own kingdom. This is because He incarnated in a human form.

Eons ago when civilization was still very young, this Nature Angel wished to incarnate in the human line of evolution. He keenly appreciated the value of human training for He came into a physical body in six successive lives. The principle which fascinated this particular Angel was the force we call love. Nature Devas develop joyousness in much the same way that love is unfolded by humanity. As the centuries progressed, the Angel who had taken these earth pilgrimages took the initiation of Lordhood which made Him a spiritual sovereign in His own kingdom. Now, because the Lord of Mt. Rainier understands human feelings, He greets every mortal who enters His aura with a ray of welcome. The whole of Rainier National Forest is a Nature Cathedral whose altar is graced by the presence of this One who has attained through fidelity and service to the Highest. These temple vibrations send their beams in every direction into those communities and cities which are near by.

The Lord of Mt. Hood is a lieutenant under the Lord of Mt. Rainier and is one of the great Lords of Nature on the Pacific Coast. His great, benign face was in, not above, the mountain on the day that we traveled in that area. He sent His welcome in the form of a white shining ball, like a diamond, that was directed to the right-hand side (the receiving side) of the car.

The pointed lesson these sacred centers disclose is that the worship of God is natural in every kingdom. Even the builders of nature's forms are striving toward an attainment in consciousness and power which is exemplified to them in the Lord of Mt. Rainier.

Were we spiritually awake we should observe the verdure of the earth peopled by beings, exquisitely small and dainty, moving in harmony with the soft, diffused music of the heavens. Forests and mountains, thought to be lonely and uninhabited, would be known to be populated by many tall, graceful beings who hover over trees, lakes and hillsides. At all times of the day the happy Sylphs of the air would be discerned, busy in their lyrical activities above the countryside. Always at the high periods of the day—dawn, noontide and sunset—would the glowing Angels of the Sun be distinguishable on the horizon.

A Tree Deva is not beautiful according to our classical ideals of beauty as its features are too elongated and narrow, its face too triangular. Yet the Angels in charge of groves of trees have an excellent equivalent of beauty—boundless and eternal energy. They appear to be light green creatures, with flashing eyes that fairly bombard one with their vitality and penetration. Frequently Devas are as tall as the trees they overshadow, though they are usually much slimmer than the tree trunk. I have spent several hours, at various times, watching a Tree

Deva move from tree to tree giving fully of his charging presence. Persons who love nature attract the attention and perchance a baptism of renewal from a Tree Deva. My friends and I always make a pilgrimage to a certain tree on a beloved mountain because to us it is "the Giving Tree," or the tree with the welcoming Deva.

In learning of the vivacious presences who pervade the outdoors, ours is the joy of inviting them into our gardens. Where they are recognized and appreciated, gardens become more healthy and luxuriant. Ordinarily Devas do not enter busy cities, so the prana is very thin in such communities.

We are permitted to ask for their blessing or protection whenever we require it. In the past, my husband and I took yearly pilgrimages into pine forests to increase our communion with the Eternal. During these sojourns, the state of the weather was a very important matter to us. Some years ago dark clouds hovered over our camp very threateningly the evening we entered the forest. The postmistress, who knew us, worried about the durability of our tent as she wrote out a campfire permit for us.

Before retirement I went outside the tent and appealed to the Angels of Rain to spare our site. All that night we heard a heavy shower falling a short distance from us, yet our camp ground was not receiving any of that downpour. On our tour of inspection the next morning we found that the entire camp had been spared but the area that surrounded it, in circular form, was rain-drenched. The postmistress, in giving us our mail, scarcely believed us when we told her that the storm had not come upon us. I believe our call for protection

133

enabled the Angels of Storm to promise us, "It shall not come nigh thee."

Rest days are very sacred to us for when they come we need their refreshment greatly. When on long lecture tours, free days usually come but once a month. One Saturday friends urged us to take our "day" with them at their cabin by a lake. As the five persons in our party entered the closed-up cottage we realized that it would take too much time to unpack and dust the living room. We agreed that the cozy veranda was the best choice of a place to spend our time. As our luncheon was being taken out of baskets and placed on the table, a very strong, mischievous wind arose. Napkins and paper plates had to be weighted to prevent their escape. After our hostess placed us, the wind became so frolicsome that our hair threatened to hide our faces. We endured discomfort for a time and then I said, "Surely this wind can be calmed so that the day can proceed harmoniously. Together let us call upon the Angels of Calm to relieve the Angels of Wind about this place." All of us closed our eyes and sent out a mental entreaty for peace. No sooner had the last person opened his eyes than a great calm enveloped us. The estate at our right and the one to our left had leaves stirring everywhere. The lake before us was somewhat choppy, yet we ate our luncheon in freedom and spent an inspired afternoon together. In taking a hike we found that the Angels of Calm followed us, for wherever we went the wind suddenly ceased. Our friends were understanding and they rejoiced with us at this evidence of Angelic care.

Now we have made our home in a wooded canyon. Questhaven Retreat is situated six miles from the nearest village. The quietness and virgin atmosphere of this six hundred and forty-acre nature sanctuary affords splendid opportunities for study of the habits and duties of those Angels of Nature in this area. Extended vision has opened the door to the wonderland of realities that exist around individuals who make their homes in rural or wilderness regions.

It was while observing the activities of the many Devas at Questhaven that we learned about King Tree Devas. In the oldest and largest live oak tree on the place is a highly advanced tree spirit, who was found to be the leader King of all the numerous tree Devas in the woods. He possesses a majestic quality of self-command, and the vitality he radiates has a stimulative effect on nearby growing things. A King Tree Deva strengthens the etheric bodies of the tallest and oldest trees in his immediate vicinity. Less developed tree spirits work on younger trees. On a few occasions the concise commands of the King Deva were heard. They were given in such a deep, resonant tone that their notes lingered in the woodland like a muted echo.

Until we lived at Questhaven we had not known that even Nature Spirits have their opposites with whom they evolve in loving harmony. The counterpart of this King Tree Deva, whom we have grown to love, is the Spirit of the Place. This order which gives service, protection, and contentment to a homesite is a feminine Nature Deva, whose ministrations bless the house, its people, and the entire property with spiritual renewal and physical guardianship.

The Angel of the Place makes her chief center in the atmosphere above a large tree near the Chapel of the

Holy Quest. Here she is to be seen most of the time. However, since the entire grounds come under her charge, this gracious spirit can be observed moving from boundary to boundary, or from the flower garden to the distant bee hives. It is this Constant Protectress who safefolds homes and land from destructive weather elements or unfriendly human beings. She also works upon the mental bodies of all whose thoughts need purification and regeneration as they enter her territory.

Questhaven's highest hill is named Inspiration Point. Above its crest can be discerned the noble Guardian of the Summit. His is the task of guiding, blessing and instructing all those beings of younger evolution who are within his domain. The King Tree Deva is his assistant. The power which emanates from a Guardian of a Mountain is changeable. We have noticed that in certain periods of the day his blessings are peaceful. At high noon they become electric in potency, and even as his influence varies, so does his position. He is always facing the sun, so in the twilight we do not see his face. One beautiful summer evening while three of us walked reverently in the groves, the Guardian of Inspiration Point uttered this blessing, "Let all the earth be at rest—peace be unto everything." On another night he distinctly prayed, "Peace and sweet rest to the world."

A lovely mountain lies two miles to the south of Questhaven. There always seems to be a mantle of stillness surrounding it. We have called this mount, which is constantly aureoled by a lavender-blue radiation, Mystic Mountain. During the day the illusive, magnetic pull of this mountainside is felt by all our observant guests. When night falls, Mystic Mountain grows lum-

inous on the higher planes. This inner Light attracts
Nature Devas from near and far. Three Guardians
stand at the entrance to the doorway of Light on the
northern slope of the range. They see that none but
those who are ready enter the open door into the cere-
monies given wholly for Nature Devas. These rituals
are in commemoration of the sun—a thanksgiving for
the light and life received throughout the day.

At unexpected moments there come to our attention
the silvery high tones of Angelic Choruses. Or we occasionally awaken to behold a day when nature is so clear
and bright that inner world doors are widely open. The
chief blessing of realizing the inner existence of all the
Angelic lives is the inspiration they arouse in us through
their selflessness, impersonality, beauty and devotion.
Human beings are not God's only creation. To know
something of His other orders expands the circle of our
enlightenment. We live in wonder and praise of the
Supreme Spirit Who made man and gave the Angelic
Kingdom charge over him. Life's manifestations are
multiformed, and each of its embodiments endeavors to
reclaim the Light, beauty and harmony once known
within the innermost.

PERFECTED BEINGS AND THEIR TASKS

LIFE is a movement toward the goal of Mastership. An evolutionary program impels the advancement, improvement and mastery of ourselves and our talents. The supreme endeavor of progress is to cause every man and every woman to become Adepts in the art of spiritual advancement and the right use of spiritual powers. Though the process is slow and gradual, from the chrysalis of preparation, after indefatigable effort, a perfected man or woman emerges.

The treasures in knowledge these Masters gathered through devious experiences and toil are the inheritance given younger souls still striving for wisdom and self-control. The benefactors, themselves, disperse their jewels; and their distributions cover an era of many centuries. In giving away the gleanings they earned by endless exertion, they thus enrich all the departments of human endeavor, and simultaneously become greater custodians of qualifications that entitle them to work within the estate of Eternal Power.

The group of Adepts who return their harvest to humanity are known as the Directors. They remain in inner communication with the earth, guiding its advancement in government, education, science, art and religion. Persons who, by their spiritual development, their devotion to world progress, and their special genius, merit masterly instruction and help, receive these advantages. How essential, therefore, are our aspirations which qualify us to work and grow under their supervision.

The Assembly of Masters seems sparse, indeed, until we consider the power invested in each Adept. Upon the advent of their Mastership, the majority of Perfected Beings enter the sixth dimension. In this region a service, which is vaster and deeper than the human mind can grasp, is rendered the Cosmos. It is sufficient to mention that the order and serenity in the universe is due partly to their united concentration.

The Great Ones who keep in touch with the affairs of the earth are the Directors previously mentioned, the Designers and the Initiators. These beings dwell in the fifth dimension, which to some is known as the Kingdom of Mind. In this region plans are conceived and prepared for execution. From here sensitive composers receive inspirations for melodic scores, while artists glimpse visions of beauty to reproduce on glorious canvases.

It is said by mystics that planets, stars and galaxies move in rhythm with the Music of the Spheres. This is true! The universe throbs with sound as fully as with life. In the outer world many creatures are articulate, but on the whole their notes are imperfect soundings. In the higher dimensions the quality of every tone is tuneful, upswinging. Waves of music flood one continually on the higher planes. There seems to be no end to their variations. At times they are silver toned and as distant as the far horizon. Again they are multisonous and resonant. Angels and men make up the invisible chorus of this permeating Spirit of Music. They do not gather in throngs to broadcast their harmony, but each sends out his tone or chant from his own sphere to add to the whole of the mighty chorale. There are beings, however, whose purpose it is to create concordant sound. They are the musicians and soloists whose adoration, through expression, forms the very soul of music. It is from the outline of their musical offerings that the world's finest works have been patterned.

When we attain realization of the Infinite Source of Life, we enter a training that prepares us for adeptship. From that time on we are under the supervision of Initiators who exert a high influence upon us. Under their watchfulness we are inspired with ideals and noble purpose. Their directions teach us to live usefully and progressively; yet, they do not solve our problems nor assume our responsibilities. Only by faithfully discharging our obligations and improving ourselves in body, mind, talent and spirit will we be able to sense their encouraging nearness.

There are seven major phases and gradations of initiation for the individual unfoldment of inherent Godliness. The first five phases are usually taken while in the physical body; the last two always occur in the higher dimensions of being. The term "initiate" applies to one who has achieved direct knowledge and consciousness of the Spirit of God. The depth of that inward realization determines the degree of initiation from which one functions in serving God's Plan. A "Master" has received the fifth initiation; a "Lord" has taken the sixth, while a "God" has concluded the seven great unfoldments of Godhood. The learned and spiritual men, Pythagoras and Lao-Tse, were Masters. The Christ Jesus and Gautama Buddha were Lords. The Bible refers to the "God," Jehovah, Who, though exceedingly advanced, is not the Spirit of God to Whom we pray.

The Masters teach that Gods must take many initiations before Their Spirits are united wholly with the Eternal Source.

Masters are supervised by Lords, and they in turn are overshadowed by the God of a particular way of unfoldment. A sixth degree initiate has the duty of radiating power, love and pure thoughts into space. His attention is given to the Cosmos; His help, to the world. Great Logi are so blended with the Spirit of God that They are channels of His Thought, His Benevolence, and His Laws which direct the world. Though the journey from passivity to conscious Godhood appears difficult and complicated, infinite simplicity, order and wisdom govern the entire process. If the thought of graded orders of Mastership be confusing, remember that the Spirit of God permeates His glorious system, that His Life is in the leaves of the trees as well as in the hearts of human beings and Godly-aware Adepts. He is nearer than our bodies, yet He simultaneously pervades the universe. Only a Supreme Infinite Divinity could have fashioned a plan whereby all life would gradually evolve, until, from a sleeping state, eternal wakefulness might embody His Creation. That the design be fulfilled, agents and artisans were necessary. Through long ages the most highly evolved of the races have been the custodians of God's Intentions. Because these Adepts are essential to the purpose of the Creator, we should desire to know as much as is possible concerning them.

The earth is supervised by the Anointed Ones who either attained Mastery here, or who are responsible for the progress of this planet. The work of administration is shared by the Masters who serve in those fields best adapted to their abilities. The Adepts do not frequently reveal themselves or their services, for only a few of them and their ministries are known.

The Great Lords send us energy, inspiration and encouragement from their high level. They seldom enter our dimension, as the Masters carry out their will for us. Amongst the Exalted Ones are the Lord Jesus, the Lord Maitreya, the Maha Chohan, the Sanat Kumara, and the Logos Osiris (the Solar Logos). Radiations from these Lords are felt very keenly on our Christmas and Easter Days, as well as during the full moon in May. The high noon period is a time when not only the Light but the silent benediction of the Solar Logos enfolds us.

The Masters in charge of the governments on our globe, about whom we know, are either guardians of nations, originators of systems, or distributors of power. The Master Ragoczy is overseer of Europe, though the various Adepts of each race assist Him considerably. The Master Morya helps direct the affairs of Asia. The director at the helm of these United States is called (after our country) the Master "Americus." Oddly, His center of power has its unseen outlet over Lincoln Memorial in Washington, D.C.

The Adept called "The Conqueror" has the most strongly developed will power of all the Great Ones interested in governmental affairs. When a nation needs to arouse its capacity for self-defense or self-preservation, this Adept becomes the hidden power behind the country's transition. At present the Conqueror is overshadowing China, due to the necessity for this nation to overcome its lethargy. India will be awakened from her inertia by the same Director.

143

A peculiar duty is that of the Master Azabar who is in charge of monetary and credit systems throughout this world. Thus far, all mediums of exchange are of experimental origin. This Adept plans to inspire a system of exchange that will not engender the dangers of selfishness and monopoly of former systems. His plan cannot be executed until a race admits a need for an improved method of exchange.

The best known Masters dedicated to the field of education are the Master Djwal Kul (also called The Tibetan), the Master Kuthumi, and the Master Elision. The Tibetan has charge of "organized thought," or established wisdoms and customs that need to be more thoroughly understood by the masses. The Master Kuthumi is devoted to the reception and spiritual radiation of the higher knowledge and trainings that are emanated in thought forms around this globe for sensitive minds or spirits to discern and utilize. The Master Elision is a woman of unusual attainment. She instructs persons who are to be sent into physical life as envoys with a particular message. Because of Her patient, serene instruction, new world movements or crusades are implanted in the fertile consciousness of souls preparing to incarnate. This imposing, beautiful Adept is sometimes contacted by Her pupils in the fifth dimension. Should these representatives forget their purpose, this Adept causes them to have an impressive dream or a spiritual vision which reawakens them to an awareness of their missions. Though there are many Adepts directing the investigations and enlightenments of science, the One best known to pupils who are in contact with Masters is the Master Hilarion. He remains closely in touch with

144

our world to encourage and inspire, by thought, those individuals who labor to create the tools of progress. Two of the common subjects now occupying the concentration and efforts of the Master Hilarion are the cure of cancer and the wider expansion of the use of radio and television.

On the path of religion are the Lord Christ Jesus, the Promised Prince, the Master John, and the Master Kuan-Yin. The Master Jesus took His sixth initiation by achieving "the ascension." Now, as the Lord Christ, He is the ruler of the spiritual impetus that is causing the inner awakenment of this humanity to an appreciation of eternal values. We have only been touched by the fringe of His influence, yet in this century alone the majority of those who love God have forsaken bigotry and intolerance for sincerity and tolerance. Under this Lord's guidance the race will undergo many changes which will bring about an open-mindedness necessary for the awakenment of the spiritual powers in man. The Lord Christ is the One in whose keeping our spiritual welfare lies. With His assistant Masters, this Anointed One, who was recently Jesus the Galilean, is endeavoring to enlighten the race, as well as to train living pupils for use in His Cause. Besides these services, His is the radiant Light which floods the inner worlds with a continuous stream of illumination and love.

The youthful Promised Prince, when seen, appears much like an artist's dream of the Boy Christ. This remarkable Adept has a merciful assignment—that of bringing about Divine intervention wherever it is merited. He is frequently felt, if not inwardly perceived, in those communities, cities or homes where tragedy stalks. When Adepts cannot avert wars, pestilence or violence caused by man's overpowering destructive thoughts, they influence men during the readjustments that follow chaos. The Promised Prince gives vision, courage, peace and gratitude to those whom His aura touches. In His presence children are happier, sweeter and more affectionate. We wonder what cause prompted this Adept to "spend His heaven doing good on earth." Our world is better for His ministry, and richer too, in spiritual contentment.

A great similarity exists between the Lord Christ and His beloved disciple, who is now an Adept, the Master John. The resemblance is more of an inner likeness than an outer one. The Lord Jesus has dark bronze-colored hair, deep brown eyes, and is dignified in bearing. The Master John has honey-colored hair, blue eyes and seems boyish despite His attainment. Yet artists have confused these Great Men, and upon their canvases have put titles pertaining to the Christ, when in reality their painting was that of the Master John. A deep bond of eternal friendship between these two Anointed Ones has engraved upon the character of the younger Master something of the transcendent beauty of His Lord.

The Master John accepts earnest seekers of reality as candidates to be prepared for world service. The progress of the neophyte causes him to be a probationer, then a disciple, and later a pupil of Masters. During these stages of inner advancement, the aspirant may experience one or several spiritual illuminations, after which he is not only a conscious servant of Adepts, but also an initiate progressing toward Mastership. "The Holy One," as the Master John is sometimes called, educates every sincere seeker in the science of spiritual self-mastery. This Adept emphasizes that character development is the first requisite essential to higher mental and spiritual achievement. After a disciple has gained self-knowledge and an honest attitude toward life, he is next enlightened as to how he may exercise the principle called *faith*, to free himself from limitations in all departments of his experience. This develops man's powers in healing, as well as in the constructive acquirement of those qualities which attract love, trust, joy, prosperity and success. These forces remain as blessings only with those who share them with as many persons as they can enfold. The disciple ever realizes that "ceasing to share, we cease to have, for such is the law of love."*

The improvement of the aspirant's efforts, realizations, and successes fits him for the more difficult feats of inner unfoldment, which the Master John discloses to those worthy of further tuition. The Master John teaches that we are not in full possession of all our God given senses. In the right season we are led to learn of the sixth and seventh senses which have their center in the realm of man's spiritual being. The sixth sense records impressions that belong to octaves of light, sound and being beyond the third dimensional existence. The Great One believes "intuition," "clairvoyance" and "clairaudience" are terms that have been profaned by improper use, yet when truly understood, they are functions of man's innate sixth sense. The seventh sense is the faculty which permits the soul to withdraw from the physical body during sleep. It likewise functions whenever the Masters deem it advisable for conscious pupils

*From Lowell's, *The Vision of Sir Launfal.*

to attend some inner conference, or take some inner initiatory work.

The Master John is but one of numerous Adepts who accept pupils. Others taking religious pupils, who are best known, are the Masters Lao-Tse, Amiel, Dratzel, Athena, Mohammed and the late Rama Krishna. The Adepts teach those of their race the principles which all Masters give to those who are worshipers of the Lord Christ. Yet, it must be remembered that all these spiritual conquerors are united by one endeavor—that of disseminating the radiance and principles of the Christ Spirit. This does not mean the doctrine the Christ Jesus gave in Palestine. The principles of the Lord Christ are far greater, vaster and deeper than those recorded in the Bible. To the fullness of the Christ message do these learned Masters bow.

In the East the Goddess Kuan-Yin receives loving homage because of Her mercy to the needy. This Being is really a Master who serves us universally from Her center in the higher dimensions. Her thoughts bring baptism and courage to the wretched in whatever state they may be manifesting. Serenely, modestly and compassionately the Master Kuan-Yin frequently enters our atmosphere to answer calls of distress. It is not the custom of this Illumined One to give attention to those who are joyous or happy, but rather to those who have lost their confidence and self-respect. There are no spiritual outcasts or souls unloved by God. The presence of such emissaries as Kuan-Yin proves how vast is the Infinite Love that envelops God's manifestation. However wrong the crimes or tragic the consequences, we find that sinners are attended by the same merciful observation given the Saints.

In the council of Perfected Men and Women is a department devoted to the subject of healing. Since the time of the Christ Jesus, the race has been urged to study and practice healing the body through the education of the mind and the strength of the spirit. Medical science, under the guidance of the Master Hilarion and His assistants, will continue its necessary work for the restoration of broken bodies. Yet, we are aware that healing can occur in the mind and spirit, but our approach to the inner healing fountain seems somewhat obscure. The Adepts who will be the exponents of our enlightenments regarding inner healing are the Master Dratzel, the Master Amiel, and the Master Mary. This latter Adept performs a great service through Her work in Lourdes.

The One who is teaching pupils the technique of spiritual healing is the Master Dratzel. He believes our illnesses are the result of our living contrary to the Divine Laws of Rhythm and Equilibrium. Activity must be of the right tempo, otherwise there is strain and chaos. Periods of quietness, for the absorption of spiritual energies, are an essential requirement. When too much activity imposes itself upon our need of peace, our inward inhalation of necessary energies is prevented. In time the Divine Spirit's government of its body is dulled; later the mind becomes erratic and the emotions unsteady. Finally, on the physical plane we find a disabled body. The Master Dratzel is now teaching those pupils who are conscious of Him, that by at-one-ment with the Reservoir of Energy, by learning to absorb healing currents in nature's sanctuary, by sane living and intelligent eating, physical well-being is assured. To those who wish to understand more about the esoteric aspect of healing, the Master Dratzel's time is dedicated. The instruction consists of teaching man how to become a channel of restorative power, and how to conduct that knowledge and influence to those who ask for it.

The Master Amiel is a strong-minded Adept, though a gentle One. His task consists of inspiring spiritually-minded persons with the secrets of the laws of vibration and how they may be used constructively in healing. This art is for the priest rather than the physician; and the complete realization of this message cannot be attained in this age, for its full revelation belongs to unborn races.

Mary, the renowned Mother of Christ Jesus, is likewise an Adept. Her interests chiefly concern woman's emancipation from unnecessary physical suffering. By Her efforts more will be made to appreciate the wisdom of birth control, and of making birth a joy instead of a delirium of pain. The Master Mary represents the Divine element of Love, and as such She is a Master of all the problems that confront women who faithfully fulfill the incentives of unselfish womanhood. Should guidance ever be required for the safety or welfare of the family life, the Master Mary is the One who will be attuned to the reception of that prayer.

The dreams and visions which weave themselves into poems, paintings and symphonies come from an exultant realm where joyousness, beauty and song are as natural to that sphere as mountains, plains and the sea are to this earth. The Master Serapis, surrounded by a host of Angelic Servers, stirs, quickens and uplifts our

150

world by charging it with thought forms which sensitive individuals receive as inspiration. We open ourselves to be elevated by something expressed truly in thought, form or tone. The passion of the Master Serapis and His numerous shining collaborators is the worship of beauty and perfection in all the arts. Persons who are aspirants on this path should pray to the Eternal Source for creative power. The Master Serapis may be attuned by the invocation, "May Infinite Inspiration for the expression of beauty, melody or reality penetrate and illumine my consciousness."

The Avatars, who are leaders of the spiritual universe, communicate with their disciples on the earth chiefly through telepathy. When their presence is necessary in our world, they come in unassuming ways. They may appear at some diplomatic conference, disguised by a very ordinary body and manner. Thus did the Master Americus mingle amongst the group who inaugurated and signed the Declaration of Independence. Their purpose in appearances of this kind is to act as a silent but thoroughly imbued magnet whose force is directed toward the accomplishment of the matter at hand.

The pupils of the Anointed Ones confront many situations of material and spiritual confusion which necessitate their control. In instances like these, certain Adepts will appear to their disciples, for the minds of the latter are apt to be too disturbed for the accurate reception of telepathic instruction. The beloved rector, Robert Norwood, had a visitation from the Christ Jesus, at a time of inner discouragement. The council of the Lord Christ, as well as the unusual inspiration of His sudden manifestation and disappearance, gave this minister the power and wisdom which made him a great and trusted man. Many are the accounts persons give who were recalled from death, who were mysteriously saved from accidents or from making wrong decisions, about a "vision" they'd had of the radiant Christ. The visions of others make all the more wonderful the actual appearance of an Initiate such as Robert Norwood experienced.

I, who write these words, do so in commemoration of a meeting with the Christ Jesus, which occurred in the high mountains. One summer morning, as I sat reveling in the beauty of nature, I heard human footsteps approaching me. Wondering who might be coming, I half arose to determine the visitor. The person I did see made me speechless, confused and unexpectedly timid all in one moment. The Man who came forward was partially hidden, at times, by trees or low limbs as He approached. Though I had frequently seen this Lord in His spiritual body, this manifestation was almost overwhelming. During the minutes that He spoke, I remained quiet, too reverent and inspired for outer speech. It is now many years since I heard that deep resonant voice, but were I blind, I'd recognize it anywhere in this vast universe. The Lord who advised me concerning the message I should give in His service, was extremely tall and very strongly built. His hair and short beard were of a bronze shade. His large eyes were a dark brown, and when He had gone, I remembered His loving but firm expression as appreciatively as I did the positive tone of joyousness and power which He vibrated. The spotless, loose white robe which He wore moved about His chest as He spoke and breathed, making me realize I was not seeing Him in a vision. At the conclusion of His instructions, He walked away as naturally as He had come. I leaned to the right to watch Him as He turned onto the road which hid Him from my view. At the time of His coming I greatly needed the strength and confidence of His orders. That strange appearance intensified my longing to bring others an awareness of the Great Ones. Words seem lifelessly inadequate when I strive to describe the transcendent glory of such a meeting.

The Masters are as varied in countenance and personality as are we who live upon this globe. The Promised Prince is a very handsome East Indian youth whose happy, loving spirit is contagious. The Masters Elision and Hilarion look like vibrant models of perfection in form. Both have wavy, chestnut-colored hair, fair skin, and blue eyes. The Lord Christ is best reflected to us by Hoffman's picture of Him, except for the sad expression the artist imagined. The Master Azabar appears more like a Westerner than a Chaldean which He was in a recent life. The Master Dratzel looks very Egyptian, for when He attained Mastership He was a high priest of Egyptian wisdom. This Adept's eyes seem black; they are piercing, probing eyes, whose influences are modified by the reserved, impersonal attitude of their possessor. In short, the Avatars look and speak like persons who were once human beings, but whose spirits were great enough to hold the lanterns of God's blessings in their services.

To one aware of the existence of Masters, all days are purposeful. He may witness many incidents that reveal an unseen guidance or an unknown director of his affairs. Spiritual progress and circumstances combine their efforts toward the discovery of the Benevolent Mentor whose existence hourly becomes more perceptible. When a Master reveals Himself to His disciple, a companionship is begun which will brighten all the days of the aspirant.

Those who are already informed of the Masters they individually follow, in the process of their instructions from the Adepts, receive advice that is difficult to practice. For instance, the Great Ones reject our adulation for our respect and trust. In all relations with aspiring students, they emphasize that a disciple is not to be dependent upon his Master, but upon himself. The Illumined Ones should be considered as our learned and kindly Brothers and Sisters. Our attitude toward them should not be meek and worshipful, but confident and respectful.

A disciple's worship belongs to God; his honor and devotion to his Master; his aspiration to the exercise of the Christ Spirit within him. For such a disciple, a day begins with the realization of God's Presence; it is motivated by service for the Master, and directed by the wisdom of the Adept's teachings. This training enables man to exert the growing powers of godliness and mastership that lie, otherwise unused, within.

Sincere students who yearn for personal confirmation as to the reality of the Masters, may do much to quicken their powers of spiritual awareness. It is surprising how much can be derived from the simple practice of thinking of the Great Ones the very first thing in the morning and the last thing at night. We must accustom ourselves to becoming "Master conscious." At high noon the influence of the Solar Logos, the Lord in charge of the sun, permeates our atmosphere and affects us strongly on the material as well as the spiritual planes. A loving, respectful salutation sent this Nature Lord greatly intensifies our reception of force from Him. In fact, the exercise of any reminder of the watchfulness of the Masters, such as periods of prayer, meditation or silence, will bring us spiritually into closer at-one-ment with them.

We cannot predict the exact moment a pilgrim of reality will contact his invincible Director, nor whether he will see the Beloved Teacher or merely feel His presence. If the time of communication could be foretold, it would occur during that period in which an aspirant's endeavors were wholly and unselfishly dedicated to the realization of God in His universe.

It is not expedient that we follow the Masters in all their movements in order to learn of them. The seed we put into the waiting soil blossoms into flowerhood whether or not we understand the laws of nature that cause these changes. Gravitation continues its good service even though we seldom, if ever, think about its effects on us. The Perfected Men and Women whose loving interest blesses our planet and all it cradles, do not require our recognition. We are the ones who must awaken to the fact that there are Selfless Benefactors working invisibly and silently carrying out the will and plan of God. Ours is the privilege of learning of them, first through the experiences of others who have known them, and second, through our own unique realizations. Though they do not ask nor urge us to join the ranks of their ministry, we have the right to offer ourselves as servants to their Divine Cause. The greatest inward happiness we can attain is that of knowing we are one of their centers of usefulness over a great network of their guidance. May our joy in realizing the existence of Masters be such a transcendent, profound and renewing awakenment that its good will reverberate to the ends of the earth for the illumination and happiness of others.